Siam

Pierre Loti, the romantic Orientalist and seductive Travel writer, describes with extraordinary pictorial skill the journey from Saigon into the interior; first along the river Mekong, at the time in flood, then through the thick forest in the heart of which is buried the ruins of Angkor-Thom, with its palaces and temples.

Pierre Loti, perhaps the world's most prolific, romantic and exotic travel writer and novelist, was born as Julien Marie Viaud in Rochefort in Western France in 1850. A childhood fascination with exotic lands across the seas led him to embark on a naval career that enabled him to seek love and adventure in many latitudes. He drew on these real life experiences when writing the romantic novels and travel books that made him one of the most popular authors of his day. Although his prolific output brought him both fame and fortune he remained a romantic escapist and never gave up his beloved naval career. He retired from the French navy in 1910 and died in 1923.

The Pierre Loti Library

THE GREAT STAIRCASE,
ANGKOR-VAT

Siam

Pierre Loti

Routledge
Taylor & Francis Group

LONDON AND NEW YORK

Published 2014 by Routledge

First published in 2002 by
Kegan Paul International

This edition first published in 2010 by
Routledge
2 Park Square, Milton Park, Abingdon, Oxfordshire OX14 4RN

Simultaneously published in the USA and Canada
by Routledge
711 Third Avenue, New York, NY 10017

First issued in paperback 2014

Routledge is an imprint of the Taylor & Francis Group, an informa business

British Library Cataloguing in Publication Data
A catalogue record for this book is available from the British Library

ISBN 978-0-710-30794-1 (hbk)
ISBN 978-1-138-86362-0 (pbk)

Publisher's Note
The publisher has gone to great lengths to ensure the quality of this reprint
but points out that some imperfections in the original copies may be
apparent. The publisher has made every effort to contact original copyright
holders and would welcome correspondence from those they have been
unable to trace.

AUTHOR'S DEDICATION

To Monsieur Paul Doumer

DEAR FRIEND,—It was during your Governorship—made notable by your so admirable talents—that last I visited Cambodia. And I owe it to your charming courtesy that I was able in a few short days to penetrate as far as Angkor. May I ask, then, that you will accept the dedication of this little narrative, as a token of my affectionate remembrance, and also of my esteem?

And will you forgive me for having said that our Empire in Indo-China would lack grandeur and, more especially, would lack stability—you who have worked so gloriously and so patiently to ensure its permanence? But so it is. I do not believe in the future of our distant colonial conquests. And I mourn the thousands and

Author's Dedication

thousands of our brave little soldiers, who,
before your arrival, were buried in those Asiatic
cemeteries, when we might so well have spared
their precious lives, and risked them only in the
last defence of our beloved French land.

PIERRE LOTI.

CONTENTS

LIST OF ILLUSTRATIONS

CHAPTER 1

SIAM

CHAPTER I

I DO not know if it is a common lot to have from childhood, as I have had, foreboding of one's whole life. Nothing has happened to me that I have not dimly foreseen from my earliest years.

The ruins of Angkor! I remember so well a certain evening of April, a little overcast, on which as in a vision they appeared to me. It was in my "museum" — a little room allotted to my childish studies at the top of my parents' house — where I had gathered together a collection of shells, rare-plumaged birds, barbaric arms and ornaments, a multitude of things that spoke to me of distant countries. For at this time it had been quite decided by my parents that I should remain at home and not venture forth into foreign lands as did my elder brother who not long before had died in the far east of Asia.

This evening then, an idle scholar as was my habit, I had shut myself in amongst these disturbing things, for reverie rather than with the idea of completing my tasks; and I was turning over some old and yellowed papers that had come back from Indo-China with the belongings of my dead brother. A few diaries. Two or three Chinese books. And then a number of I know not what colonial review in which was recounted the discovery of colossal ruins hidden in the depths of the forests of Siam.

There was one picture at which I stopped with a kind of thrill—of great strange towers entwined with exotic branches, the temples of mysterious Angkor! Not for one moment did I doubt but that one day I should see them in reality, through all and notwithstanding all, in spite of prohibitions, in spite of impossibilities.

To think of it better I moved to the window of my museum and gazed, chin in hand, at the outstretched country. Of all the windows in the house this one of mine commanded the most distant prospect. In the foreground were the old roofs of the tranquil neighbourhood; beyond, the hundred-year-old trees of the ramparts, and then, and at last, the river by which the ships made their way to the ocean.

And very distinctly at this time there came to me a foreknowledge of a life of travels and adventures, with hours magnificent, even a little fabulous as for some oriental prince ; and hours, too, infinitely miserable. In this future of mystery, greatly magnified by my childish imagination, I saw myself becoming a kind of legendary hero, an idol with feet of clay, fascinating thousands of my fellow-creatures, worshipped by many, and by some suspected and shunned.

In order that my personality might be more romantic there needed some shadow in the renown I was imagining for myself. What could that shadow well be ? Something fantastic —something fearsome ? Perhaps a pirate. Yes ; it would not greatly have displeased me to be suspected of piracy on seas far distant and scarcely known.

And then there appeared to me my own decline, and, much later, my return to the scenes of my childhood, with heart aweary and whitening hair. My parental home, piously conserved, would have remained unaltered ; but here and there, pierced in the walls, hidden doors would

lead to a palace of the Arabian nights, filled
with the precious stones of Golconda, with all
my fantastic booty. And then, for the Bible
was at that time my daily reading, I heard
murmuring in my brain the verses of Ecclesiastes
on the vanity of things.

Tired of the sights of the world and entering
again, an old man, the same little museum of
my childhood, I was repeating to myself: "I
have tried all things; I have been everywhere;
I have seen everything. . . ." And amongst
the many phrases already ringing sadly that
came to lull me at my window was one that,
I know not why, will remain for ever impressed
upon my memory. It was this: "In the depths
of the forests of Siam I have seen the star of
evening rise over the ruins of Angkor."

A whistle, at once commanding and soft,
caused me suddenly to become again the little
submissive child that in reality I had not ceased
to be. It came from below, from the courtyard
with its old walls garlanded with plants. I
would have known it amongst a thousand; it was
the usual summons of my father when I was
discovered in some small transgression. And
I replied, "I am up here, in my museum. Do
you want me? Shall I come down?"

Siam

He should have come into my study and cast his eye over my unfinished lessons.

"Yes, come down at once, little man, and finish your Greek composition, if you want to be free after dinner to go to the circus."

(I used to love the circus; but I was toiling that year under the ferule of a hated professor whom we called the Great Black Monkey, and my over-long tasks were never done.)

Still, I descended to set myself to the composition. The courtyard, that yet was pleasant enough with its old low walls overgrown with roses and jasmine, struck me as narrow, as too enclosed, and the April twilight falling at this hour seemed unwontedly cloudy, even some- how sinister; in my mind I had a vision of blue skies, wide spaces, the open sea—and the forests of Siam, out of which rose from amongst the palms the towers of prodigious Angkor.

CHAPTER II

CHAPTER II

Saturday, 23rd November 1901.

IT is some five-and-thirty years later. A warm, heavy, torrential rain is pouring from leaden-coloured clouds, deluging the trees and streets of a colonial town that smells of musk and opium. Half-naked Annamites and Chinese hasten along, by the side of our homebred soldiers whose faces are pale beneath their cork helmets. A noxious moist heat afflicts the lungs; the air might be the vapour of some cauldron in which perfumes were mingled with the odours of putrefaction.

And this is Saigon—a town I could have wished that I might never see, of which the very name once seemed to me mournful. For it was hither that my brother (my senior by fifteen years) had come, like so many others of his generation, to take the germs of death.

To-day this Saigon of exile and languor is a familiar place enough. After an acquaintance

of many years I have come now to think that
I no longer hate it. When I came to it for
the first time—already a little past the prime of
life—how sadly strange and unfriendly I found
its welcome. But I have grown used to its
leaden skies, to the exuberance of its unhealthy
verdure, to the Chinese quaintness of its flowers,
to its loneliness in the midst of grassy plains
sown with tombs, to the little cat's eyes of its
yellow women, to all that constitutes its morbid
and perverse attraction. Besides, I have already
memories here, a semblance of a past; almost I
have loved here; here, too, I have had my share
of suffering. And to the immense cemetery,
overgrown with rank herbage, I have led many
of my comrades-in-arms.

On the occasions of my previous visits we
were in a state of continual alarms, in connection
with warlike expeditions into Annam and Tonkin
and China; and it had not been possible to find
time to make the deep plunge into the interior
of the country, towards the ruins of Angkor.
But at last, for once, I find myself at Saigon
and at leisure. Our period of active service had
terminated in the gulf of Pekin, and the grim
warship to which I am attached is anchored here
certainly for more than a month, alongside the

Siam

homesick quay, near to that dismal and, as it might seem, abandoned dockyard, where the earth is red as bloodstone beneath foliage that is too magnificently green.

And this evening, after so many years of waiting, I set out at length on my visit to the great ruins. The rain pours down on Saigon in the customary deluge. Everything is streaming with the tepid water. The carriage which takes me to the railway (even in so commonplace a fashion does my journey begin) throws up waves of reddish-coloured mud on to the naked bodies and the white linen clothes of passers-by. Around the station is a quarter that might be in China itself, instead of in a French colony.

The train starts; the carriages are stifling in spite of the visit of the storm. In the twilight, which gathers apace under the heavy clouds, we have to traverse melancholy stretches of grass-land which are studded with a multitude of old Chinese mausoleums of the colour of rust; the whole extent of the " Plain of Tombs," where already things lose their colour and become grey; and, were it not for the persistent heat, this November evening on this foreign steppe would be like one of our more misty evenings at home. And then the night

13

overtakes us in the endless succession of the ricefields.

At the end of a two hours' journey the train stops. We are at Mytho, which is the terminus of the line, the end of this unpretentious little colonial railway. Here the scene changes, as happens commonly in this region. The clouds have melted from the sky, and the nocturnal blue stretches limpid, wonderful, with its sowing of stars. We are in the neighbourhood of a large, tranquil river, the Mekong; hard by here a steamboat should be waiting to take me, first of all, to Cambodia, by way of the river. The road which leads me to the spot, along the bank of the river, is like the avenue of some trim park, only the trees that overhang it with their branches are larger than ours, and fireflies everywhere flicker their nimble, dancing fires. Peace and silence. The place would be perfect were it not for the eternal heaviness of the air and the enervating perfumes. A number of lights in row amongst the greenness indicate the streets, or rather the alleys, of the humble provincial town, which was laid out in a single planning on the level plain. And how can one describe the sadness, the brooding pensiveness, in the night-time, of these corners of France, of these outposts of the fatherland astray in the thick bushland of Asia, isolated from everything, even from the sea ? . . . Little groups of soldiers in white linen uniforms are taking their monotonous evening stroll along the road I am following, and, as they pass, I can detect in their voices now the accent of Gascony, now the accent of my own native province. Poor fellows! the mothers that bore them are waiting anxiously at far distant firesides; while they, perforce, must squander here a year or two of the most precious of life. Perhaps they will leave behind them little half-bred tokens of their being, who little by little may infiltrate the French blood into this stubborn yellow people; then they will return home, with blood for long impoverished by the sojourn in this climate; or, perhaps, they will not return, but lay their bones, like so many thousand others, in the red earth of the neighbouring cemeteries—which are disquieting in that they are so vast, and so overgrown with rank weeds.

The steam-boat gets under way as soon as I am on board; we begin to ascend the Mekong, keeping near to the banks, where the trees seem to stretch out a curtain intensely black, and the fireflies continue their sparkling dances. Before we reach the border of the forests of Siam, we shall have to traverse the whole of Cambodia; but I purpose stopping at Pnom-Penh, the capital of the good king Norodom, where I shall arrive by to-morrow night.

CHAPTER III

CHAPTER III

Sunday, 24th November 1901.

MY little steam-boat has been making way all night against the current of the majestic river, journeying towards the north. Daybreak finds us continuing the same peaceful navigation through this Indo - Chinese bush, the endless curtains of which were so black under the stars, but are become glorious now in the sunlight. Banana - palms, cocoanut - palms, mangroves, bamboos, rushes, packed close together in a serried and endless mass. At first sight one might think the country was uninhabited; but looking more closely one sees clearly enough how cunningly its opulent green mantle has been penetrated underneath by the human microbe. Here and there tracks, such as might be made by the beasts of the forest, debouch from beneath the trees and lead to the river. They are the first indication of the villages. As we pass them at close quarters, the perfumes of the flowers become mingled with offensive animal odours; a few poor huts are disclosed, cowering among the branches, and human beings appear, lowly and, as it were, negligible, under the sovereign eternal verdure. Lean Annamites with bodies of the colour of saffron. Young women often pleasing in body and countenance, but repulsive as soon as they smile and show their teeth lacquered in black, which make the mouth look like a gloomy cave. A diminutive humanity, at once infantine and old, which has scarcely evolved since the time of the prehistoric ancestor, and has been hidden for centuries in the foliage of this tropical flora.

There are a number of native canoes on the river, fashioned each one of them out of a hollowed tree-trunk; and everywhere along the banks primitive kinds of fishing-tackle— wattle-like things made of reeds or bamboo. For the most part they resemble huge cocoons, which, as they emerge from the green confusion, plunge at once half-way into the water. You might almost imagine that they were the chrysalides out of which these little yellow people were born: a sort of worm or maggot, whose business it was here to gnaw the wonder-

COCOANUT PALMS

ful covering of the plains. And over and above the so many outspread snares are the innumerable bird-fishers, long-legged, long-necked, with long, cruel beaks always ready for their prey. Men and wading birds alike waylay the myriads of silent, rudimentary lives which pass within the river. From all antiquity their flesh has been nourished on the colder flesh of fish.

More than once my pilot loses his way in the winding of these banks, so endlessly alike, and strays into deceptive little tributaries, bordered always with the same curtains of verdure. And we get stranded there and have to make our way back.

As evening approaches the human type changes. The few inhabitants of the banks, of whom we get glimpses through the reeds, are more Hindoo, more Aryan in type; their eyes are large and *straight*, and the eyebrows well marked; moustaches shadow the lips of the men. The habitations also are different, higher and raised on piles. We are no longer in Cochin-China. We have entered Cambodia.

And an hour after midnight we moor our boat to a quay before the town of Pnom-Penh, which is asleep under the stars.

CHAPTER IV

CHAPTER IV

THE air here is already less oppressive than at
Saigon, less charged with electricity and moisture.
One feels more alive.

And a melancholy of a different kind emanates
from this town, lost as it is in the interior of a
land - bound country, without ships, without
sailors, without animation of any sort. It is
comparatively but a few years since King
Norodom confided his country to France, and
already everything that we have built at Pnom-
Penh has taken on an air of old age under the
scorching of the sun. The fine straight roads
we traced here, along which no one passes, are
green with weeds. It might be one of those
ancient colonies, the charm of which lies in
desuetude and silence.

To-day, nevertheless, is the third day of the
traditional water festival, and in the evening, as
the sun turns to a coppery red, the banks of the

river suddenly become animated. In one of the royal junks, the prow of which represents the enormous head of some monster of Cambodian dream, I watch, in company with a score or so French men and women living in exile here at Pnom-Penh, the progress of the long racing canoes. They go past in a furious eddy of spray, manipulated by half-nude men, who paddle standing, with movements of dexterous grace, shouting, at the same time, encouraging cries.

CHAPTER V

CHAPTER V

Tuesday, 26th November 1901.

STANDING back from the bank of the river
stretch the vast quarters of the King, invested
in silence. With their denuded courts they
form, as it were, a kind of glade in the midst of
this country, by the side of this town so overgrown with trees, and the roads of reddish
earth which surround them are pitted with
large imprints from the daily promenade of the
elephants.

This morning at half past six o'clock, wandering alone in the early sunshine, I enter the gate
of one of the courtyards of the palace—a courtyard of considerable extent, paved in white. In
the middle, isolated in the bare emptiness, is a
slim pagoda of white and gold, the roof of
which bristles with golden spikes, and isolated
also at either side of this little solitude two
high bell-turrets of gold, extraordinarily pointed,
which are supported on a kind of rock-work,
decked with orchids and a diversity of rare

blooms. I perceive no sign of living thing. But the silence here is of a peculiar kind; a sound as of rustling mingles with it in an undertone without disturbing it—a vague, aerial music which at first escapes definition; it is the concert of the little silver bells suspended at each point of the bell-turrets and of the roofs; the least breath of air that passes makes them tinkle softly.

The pagoda, which is quite new, is resplendent in the whiteness of its marble and its glistening golds. Its windows are decorated with copings of gold, which, against the white background of the wall, stand out like pieces of fine jewellery. Its roofs, covered with gilded ceramics, are ornamented at each corner with horns of extraordinary length, which curve and recover, menacing in all directions. Compared with these the horns of the Chinese pagodas seem verily only rudimentary things, little better than shoots; many giant bulls, one is tempted to say, have been uncoifed to decorate this strange temple. The different peoples of the yellow race have been haunted for centuries by this conception of horned roofings for their religious edifices, but it has been left to the Cambodians to surpass them all in extravagance.

Siam

Steps are approaching, heavy steps, and three elephants appear. Paying no heed to me they cross the courtyard with an intelligent, business-like air, as of people who know what they have to do. The sound of their march and of the bells hung at their collars breaks for a moment into the æolian concert which falls discreetly from above, and then, as soon as they have gone, the musical silence returns — a silence which is exquisite here in the purity and comparative freshness of the morning.

The open doors of the pagoda invite me to enter.

On its ceiling, on its walls, golds of extraordinary brilliance glisten everywhere, and my footsteps resound on flags of bright new silver with which the pagoda is paved throughout. There are still countries then, where, even in our times, men think to build such sanctuaries!

Almost immediately, through a different door, there enter four small creatures, all of them young, all of them slender, with hair cut short like boys, and a gardenia bloom fastened over the ear. The beautiful silks which cover them, outlining their scarcely-formed breasts, indicate them to be women of the palace—dancing girls beyond a doubt, for there is scarcely any other womankind at the court of old King Norodom. To the movement which I make to withdraw they reply by a charming, timid sign, as if to say : " Pray, stay where you are ; you are not disturbing us." And I thank them with a bow. This human courtesy which we have learnt at opposite ends of the earth, and of which just now we have made distantly, as it were, the exchange, is, perhaps, the only notion we have in common. In the course of my life I had met with many women of this type, women who, in their relation to life, are little better than dolls or toys, but never before had I come across the little Cambodian *at home*; and I watch with interest these four as, with silent step and easy, unaffected grace, they move about over the silver floor. From early childhood their bodies, their every limb, have been made supple by those long, ritual dances, which are the custom here on feast days and days of funeral. What is it brings them so early to the temple ? What childish scruple ? And what can be the nature of the prayers formulated by their little souls, that are revealed now, anxious, in their eyes ?

The heat is already oppressive as I return

to the quarters occupied by the French, to look
for shade on board my little steamboat moored
against the bank. Prostration and silence in the
streets, so straightly made but so empty, where
the weeds encroach upon the footpaths. Save
for some naked Cambodian slaves, who, careless
and happy, are watering the lawns of the
strangely-flowered gardens, I meet nobody.
The capital of King Norodom has gone to
sleep till the close of the day, under the dazzling
brilliance of the sun. And clearly one gets the
impression that this little corner of France,
which has been grafted here, will not endure,
will not "make good," such an air of antiquity
and abandonment has it taken on after a few
short years.

At three o'clock in the afternoon I make
ready to continue my journey towards the ruins
of Angkor, against the current of the Mekong.

Pnom-Penh disappears at once; and the prodigious Asiatic bush envelops us again within
its profound curtains. At the same time there
is revealed, everywhere around, an animal life
of extraordinary intensity. On the banks,
which we almost brush in passing, whole armies
of bird-fishers are standing on the watch:
pelicans, egrets, and marabouts. Frequently

the air is blackened with flights of crows. In the distance arise little clouds of green-coloured dust, which as they approach are seen to be flights of innumerable paroquets. Here and there the trees are full of monkeys, and you can see the long tails hanging in lines like a fringe on all the branches.

From time to time, human habitations in an isolated group. Always a long shaft of gold dominates them, pointing into the sky — the pagoda.

My men having asked that they might be allowed to provision themselves with fruits for the journey, I call a halt, at the hour of twilight, at a large village built on piles right on the bank of the river. Some smiling Cambodians come forward at once offering fresh cocoa-nuts and bunches of bananas. And while the bargaining proceeds, an enormous red moon rises beyond, over the infinitude of the forests.

Night falls as we resume our journey. Cries of owls, cries of beasts of prey, an infinite concert of all kinds of musical insects, delirious with the frenzy of the night-time in the inextricable verdure.

And then, later on, the waters expand so that we no longer see the banks. We are enter-

Siam

ing the immense lake formed here every year
by the potent river, which periodically inundates
the low-lying plains of Cambodia and a part of
the forests of Siam.   Not a breath of wind.
As if we were floating on oil, we trace, in
gliding over this fever - breeding lake, smooth
folds which the moon silvers.   And the warm
air, which we cleave rapidly in our progress,
is encumbered with clouds of giddily - circling
insects, which assemble in a regular vortex at
the sight of our lanterns, and fall upon us
like rain: gnats, mosquitoes, day-flies, beetles,
dragon-flies.

About midnight, when we had retired for the
night, and lay, half-dressed, with the windows
open, we were visited without warning by a
swarm of large, black beetles, covered with
prickles like a chestnut, but otherwise inoffen-
sive, which crawled very rapidly over us, ex-
ploring our chest and arms.

CHAPTER VI

CHAPTER VI

Wednesday, 27th November 1901.

ON the lake, large as a sea, behold the rising
of the sun. And in a few minutes everything
takes on colour. The eastern horizon becomes
suffused with pink, and a line of beautiful
Chinese green indicates the endless continua-
tion of the inundated forest. By way of contrast
on the western horizon—where the shore is too
far off to be seen—there is a massing of sombre,
chaotic, terrifying things, which seem to weigh
upon the waters—things which hold together
and remain in position, as do the heapings of
mountains, and stand out as clearly as real
mountain summits against the clear sky; but
which seem, nevertheless, to be on the point of
toppling in downfalls as formidable as those of
the end of the world. And the whole of this
heaped-up mass is ravined and caverned and
contorted, with deep shadows in its folds, and
lights of reddish copper on its prominences.

And right above it, as if it had been placed there, the old, dead moon, a large full moon of the colour of tin, begins to fade before the sun which rises opposite. All this western horizon would be a sight from which to avert the eyes, a sight to strike terror, did one not know what in fact it is : a storm, of an aspect a hundred times more terrible than ours, which broods there as if sleeping, and in all probability will not break.

It was to this we owed the heat and the kind of electric tension so enervating in its effect, which had oppressed us towards the end of the night. From experience of these climates we had guessed before seeing it that somewhere or other in the air there was a monster of the kind. But as we watch it begins to lose shape, to become attenuated so that it no longer has the appearance of consistence, and we breathe more and more freely in proportion as it all gradually dissolves. At the moment there are a few negligible clouds ; presently there remains nothing but a light vapour which does no more than cover with a warm mist the western side of this little sea over which we travel alone.

Not a canoe in sight, no more sign of man than before his first appearance amongst the terrestrial fauna. But here and there long trails of a pinkish-white streak the greenish waters saturated with organic substances. They are companies of pelicans, sleeping as they float.

Until the middle of the day, we continue our progress over this motionless lake, which gleams like polished tin. On the eastern horizon what looks to be a kind of green foam stretches endlessly, and with an endless sameness: tall trees, the trunks of which are entirely submerged, so that the tops alone rise out of the water. It is only an illusory shore, for beneath the verdure the lake continues its extent for indefinite distances. It is no more than the boundary of the deeper waters in which the vegetation has lost its footing.

Thirty leagues, forty leagues of submerged forest unroll in this way while we continue our peaceful course towards the north. An immense zone, useless during this season from the point of view of man, but a prodigious reservoir of animal life. Shades full of snares and ambushes, of ferocious beaks and claws, of little venomous teeth, of little stings, sharpened for deadly stingings. There are branches that bend beneath the weight of grave marabouts in repose; and trees so laden with pelicans that in the distance they look to be abloom with large pale-pink flowers.

When, in the course of our navigation, we draw close to this forest of eternal green, so as almost to touch it, the hosts of the branches become alarmed and take to flight. And then, at close quarters, we see what can only be described as skeins of creeping plants wound, as it were, round the trees, binding them one to another, so that the forest presents itself to us as one single inextricable mass.

At about one o'clock, we cast anchor in the shade of a little bay, enclosed with wanton verdure. This, it appears, is the place where the large sampans, ordered in advance from the chief of the nearest village, on the way to Angkor, will come to find me. The little steam-boat which has carried me to this point would not in any case be able to proceed further through the forest.

They appear at about six o'clock in the evening, these roofed sampans, emerging one after the other from under the medley of creepers. The large red sun has just set when I take my place in one, with my French servant, my Cambodian interpreter, my Chinese boy, and our light travellers' baggage. And then,

THE BEGINNING OF THE RAINS

propelled by the native rowers, we begin to thrust our way into the labyrinth of trees, into the heart of the submerged forest which closes over us. At the same time the night comes to envelop us, almost suddenly, without any period of twilight.

The region which we are now about to traverse is transformed into a lake only for about six months of the year. Soon the waters will subside, and the earth will re-appear and proceed hastily to cover itself with herbage. And men will return to build their huts for the dry season, leading back their flocks and followed by the inevitable train of tigers and monkeys. A pastoral life will resume its place here until the next rains.

All these large trees, immersed up to the spreading of the branches, are not distinguishable in the darkness from our oaks and beeches; and it might be an inundated country of a climate such as our own, were it not for this oppressive heat, this excess of perfumes, this excess of rustling round about, this plethora of sap and life. The sky is covered anew with storm-clouds, and the atmosphere again becomes almost stifling. The night is without stars and without moon. In this zone where we are now, there are no silhouettes of palms. The great black tufts which follow one another in an endless procession during the course of our progress are like the tops of our trees at home, although they are of unknown species. Despite the night you can see them repeated in the darkened mirror of the waters, and their reversed reflections somehow seem to reinforce the feeling of inundation, of something abnormal, of cataclysm, that impresses itself upon you. Continually, as we go along, we hit against the thick foliage, and lizards that were lying asleep, day-flies in myriads, little serpents and locusts descend upon us. Often our rowers lose their way, call to one another with mournful Asiatic cries, and change their course. The ruins which we are going to visit are truly admirably guarded by such a forest as this.

At the end of some two hours, however, we succeed in emerging from beneath the trees, and enter a kind of marsh, amongst reeds and grasses of extraordinary size. Here we find a narrow river which we commence to ascend, brushing against reeds and plants of every sort. The night grows darker and darker. As we pass we disturb great birds which take to flight, or perhaps an otter, or some unknown beast which we can hear making its escape with light nimble bounds.

And at last, at about ten o'clock, while our boatmen continue their rowing without a stop, we stretch ourselves under our mosquito-nets and fall at once into a trustful sleep.

CHAPTER VII

CHAPTER VII

IT is about two o'clock in the morning. We are awakened, but deliciously and scarcely, by a sound of music, slow, soft, never before heard, and of a wonderful strangeness. It sounds neither too far off nor too near — flutes, dulcimers, zithers, and, it would seem, too, peals of little bells and silver gongs rhythming the melody in an undertone. At the same time we become conscious that the music of the oars has ceased and the sampan no longer moves. Here, then, is the end of our journey by water, and we are moored, no doubt, against the bank ready to disembark as soon as the sun rises. The music continues, monotonous, repeating over and over again the same phrases, which yet are not wearisome but soothing. And we soon fall asleep again, after murmuring to ourselves, in these moments of half-waking: "Good! We have reached Siam . . .

at some village . . . and there is a nocturnal festival . . . in the pagoda . . . in honour of the local gods. . . . "

Half-past six o'clock in the morning. We awake again, but for good this time, for it is day. Between the planks which shelter us we see filtering rays of pink light. The music has not ceased. It is there still—always soft and always the same, but mingled now with the shrill clarion of cocks, and the sounds of the daily life about to recommence.

It is a positive enchantment to gaze outside. If the vegetation of the submerged forest, on which our eyes closed, recalled that of our climate, here a tropical flora of the utmost extravagance is displayed in all varieties of palms, of huge green plumes, of huge green fans. We are before a village, on a little river with flowery banks. Through the reeds the rising sun shoots everywhere its golden arrows. Little thatched houses built upon piles make a line along a pathway of fine sand. Men and women, half-nude, slender, with bodies copper-coloured, come and go amongst the verdure. They pass and pass again, a little out of curiosity, perhaps; but their curiosity is not impertinent, and their eyes are smiling and kindly. The flowers shed

Siam

a surpassing fragrance : an odour of jasmine, of gardenia, of tuberose. In the clear light of the broadening day this simple coming and going of the morning seems like a scene of the early ages, when tranquillity was still the lot of man. And, too, used as we had become to the ugliness of the daughters of Annam, who see only through cramped eyelids, through two little oblique slits, what a change it seems, and what a comfort, to come amongst a people who open their eyes more or less as we open our own.

And we put foot to earth — in Siam.[1] Beyond, under a hangar with a roof of mats, the musicians of the night, who for the moment have ceased to play, are squatting by the side of their dulcimers, their flutes, and their zithers. They had given all this concert of theirs in honour of some humble Buddhist pictures— poor daubs of blue and red and gold, which are hung there ; before which also are fading offerings of flowers: lotus, jasmine, and water-lilies.

And now arrive my ox-carts, ordered

[1] The writer knows, of course, that under an arrangement recently made with Siam the territory of Angkor has been ceded to Cambodia—in other words, to France.

since yesterday from the chief of the district; five carts, be it understood, for there is not room in one for more than a single person, who sits back to back with the driver. They resemble a sort of mandoline, mounted on wheels and drawn by the arm, which is curved like the prow of a gondola.

We have to hasten our departure in order that we may arrive at Angkor before the heat of mid-day. At the outset of our journey we follow the course of the narrow river along a path-way of sand, bordered with reeds and flowers. Above us is a colonnade of tall cocoa-nut-palms, from which hang garlands of creepers, decked with clusters of flowers. There is an exquisite morning freshness under these high trees. We pass through villages, peaceful and pleasing as in the golden age, where the inhabitants watch us go by with smiles of shy good-will. The presence of an Indian strain in the blood of these people becomes more and more pronounced, and many of the women have large, black eyes, shaded by lashes that might be the envy of a Bayadère.

At the end of about an hour we stop at Siem-Reap, almost a town, but quite Siamese in character, with its little houses raised always

on piles, and its pagoda bristling with golden
horns. It boasts a post office, however, quite
a countryside post office, where one may frank
letters with stamps bearing the likeness of King
Chulalongkorn; and a little telegraph office
also, for a telegram is brought to me, couched
in this wise :

"Superior Resident at Pnom-Penh to the
Governor of Siem-Reap. Will you please
inform M. Pierre Loti that he will find four
elephants at Kompong-luong on his return."

It is what I was hoping for. I had asked
the good King Norodom if he could place four
elephants at my disposal in order that, when I
had made the pilgrimage to Angkor, I might
visit the pagoda where rest the ashes of the
queen-mother of Cambodia, in the midst of
forest.

On leaving Siem-Reap our ox-carts turn
away from the river and follow another sandy
road which plunges right into the forest. And
then suddenly there is an end to the tall green
palms above our heads; for all this vegetation
of cocoanut and areca palms is confined to
the banks of the river. We make our way
now under foliage that is similar to that of

our own climate, only the trees that bear it would be a little giantlike compared with ours. In spite of so much shade the heat, as the sun climbs the sky, becomes every minute more oppressive. Following the ill-defined road through the high forest trees and impenetrable bush, our carts jog along in time with the trotting of the oxen between two banks of thicket or bracken. And the prudent monkeys cling to the highest of the branches.

When, at the end of some two hours' travelling through the forest in this fashion, we were beginning, what with the jolting and the rocking and the heat, to feel ourselves overtaken by somnolence, the fabulous town itself was suddenly revealed to our eyes.

Before us there is gradually unfolded an extent of open space; first of all a marsh overgrown with grasses and water-lilies, then a wide stretch of water which liberates us at last from the forest, in the dense covering of which we had been travelling; and, further on, beyond the stagnant waters, a number of towers, in the form of tiaras, towers of grey-coloured stone, immense dead towers, outlined against the pale luminosity of the sky. Yes! I recognise them at once. They are indeed the towers of the old picture which had so troubled me once upon a time, on an April evening, in my little museum. I am in the presence of mysterious Angkor!

And yet somehow I do not feel the emotion that I should have expected. I come to them too late in life, perhaps; or perhaps I have seen too many of these remains of the great past, too many temples, too many palaces, too many ruins. Besides it is all so blurred, as it were, under the glare of the sun; one sees it ill by reason of the very excess of light in the sky. And, above all, midday is drawing near with its lassitude, its invincible somnolence.

The colossal ramparts and the towers that have just appeared to us, like some mirage of the torrid heat, are not the town itself, but only Angkor - Vat, its principal temple. The town, Angkor-Thom, so we are advised, lies further away, immense and indeterminate, buried under the tropical forest.

Leading to this phantom basilica is a bridge of remote ages, built of cyclopean blocks, which crosses a pool or moat, choked with reeds and water-lilies. Two monsters, corroded by time and bearded with lichen, guard the entrance to it. It is paved with long flagstones, which sink and slope, and in places seem almost on the point of slipping into the greenish waters. Drawn by our oxen we cross it at a foot's pace, almost asleep. On the further side opens a gateway, surmounted by turrets like tiaras, and flanked by two gigantic cobra serpents which rear up and display, in the form of a fan, their seven heads of stone.

And, having passed through this gateway, we are within the outer walls, which have a circumference of more than a league: a mournful, enclosed solitude, resembling a neglected garden, with brambles entwined with fragrant jasmine, out of which rise, here and there, ruins of little towers, statues with closed eyes, and the multiple heads of the sacred cobra.

The sun is scorching now that we have left the shade of the thick branches. An avenue paved with grey-coloured stones stretches before us its diminishing line, leading straight to the sanctuary, the gigantic mass of which now dominates everything. A sinister kind of avenue it seems, passing thus through a little desert, strangely mysterious, and leading to ruins under a sun of death. But as we draw nearer to this temple, which we had thought vowed to a perpetual silence, a sound of soft music comes

more and more clearly to our ears, which are a
little bothered, if the truth be told, by the
feverish heat and the longing for sleep. For
all that it is clearly a sound of music, distinct
from the concert of the insects and the creaking of our ox-carts. It resembles vaguely the
sound of innumerable human voices chanting a
slow psalmody. Who can they be that sing
thus amongst the ruins in spite of the over-
powering heaviness of mid-day ?

At the very foot of this crushing mass of
sculptured stone, of terraces and stairways, and
towers that soar into the sky, we come upon
the village from which these chanted prayers
proceed. Overhung by tall, frail palm-trees are
a few little houses on piles, constructed very
lightly of wood and mats, with elegant little
festooned windows which are quickly adorned
with curious heads at the sound of our approach.
The heads are those of persons with shaven
polls, who are clothed each of them in a lemon-
coloured robe, beneath an orange - coloured
drapery. They chant in a subdued voice, and
continue to watch us without interrupting their
tranquil litany.

It is a very singular village this, without
women, without cattle, without cultivation,

nothing but these singers, yellow in face, and clothed in two shades of yellow. About two hundred monks from Cambodia and Siam, dedicated to the guardianship of the sacred ruins, live there in continual prayer, chanting night and day before this heaped-up mountain of titanic stones.

The arrival of our carts, however, and our oxen and drivers interrupts for a moment their peaceful contemplation. To give us welcome two from amongst them descend from their perched-up houses, and, with polls shining in the sunlight, advance to meet us, without haste or embarrassment, in the overpowering heat which now falls perpendicularly upon the earth, and which the earth gives back with added unwholesomeness and moisture.

They offer us as lodging the large shelter provided for the use of the faithful during the pilgrimages. Raised on piles like the houses, it consists of a kind of open-work floor with a roof of thatch supported by pillars of reddish wood. It boasts no wall, and to screen us, night and day, we have only the transparent curtains of our mosquito nets. By way of furniture there is nothing but an old Buddhist altar, with gods of fading gold, before which little heaps of

HABITATIONS OF THE MONKS, ANGKOR-VAT

ashes attest the burning of many a perfumed twig.[1]

We lie down there on mats, behind the muslin curtains which have been hastily hung, happy to be able at last to stretch ourselves some five or six feet above the ground where the snakes crawl, happy to feel that our heads are protected by a veritable roof, under which there is, if not coolness, at least a deep shade. And seeking the shade also, the oxen lie down beneath our dwelling, on the moist, warm earth.

If there had been any air it would have come to us from all parts, even from below, for the very floor is open. But there is none anywhere at this hour when everything is burning, motionless and languid. In the midday torpor all sounds subside, and things themselves become, as it were, congealed. The eternal psalmody of the monks, even the murmur of the insects seem to be muted and to abate. Through the muslin, as through a fog, we still see, quite close, disconcertingly close, the enormous base of the temple, the towers of

[1] I am informed that since Angkor came into the possession of France a house has been built after the fashion of an Indian bungalow for the accommodation of visitors from Europe.

which we can imagine vanishing above in the white incandescence.

The heaviness and the mystery of these immense ruins disquiet me more in measure as my eyes close, and it is only when sleep is on the point of making me lapse into unconsciousness that I recognise as finally accomplished my hope of long ago, that I realise that I have in fact arrived before the ruins of Angkor.

I must have been asleep some two or three hours when by degrees consciousness returned to me. What can I have been dreaming of? I seemed to be in a nameless country, where everything was mournful and dark. Near me, on a pale whitish strand, before a sea confused and black, were moving the silhouetted shapes of human beings, whom, perhaps, I may have loved in some previous existence—who can tell? —for I am conscious almost of a pang, when the broad light of reality, returning suddenly, drives them into a non-existence beyond recall. Where am I? In what region of the earth do I re-open my eyes? The air is hot with a moist, close heat, as if I had been lying above a basin of boiling water. There is shade above my head, but around me, framed by this kind of fringe which falls from the thatched roof, are adjacent

ANGKOR-VAT

things which shimmer in an excess of vivid light: foliage bathed in sunshine, and interminable rows of grey stones, the reflection of which dazzles me. And in the air there is a sound of chanting, a kind of lamentation in an unknown rhythm. And then I remember—it is the litany of the monks; and these grey stones are the eternal courses of the ruins. I have been sleeping since midday at the foot of the temple of Angkor, in this clearing, guarded by moats and low walls, and surrounded on all sides in an eternal silence by the thick, green shroud of the tropical forest.

It is half-past three, the hour when everything awakes here, after the daily prostration. Beneath the open-work floor I can hear the oxen moving, and the drivers beginning again to talk. The flies buzz in a crescendo, and the chanting of the monks grows louder.

There is no cloud in the sky, no menace of any sort. The whole vault is resplendent, palely blue, above the enormous towers. There seems no doubt but that the rain is going to spare us for the afternoon. Let us, then, put the oxen again to the carts; instead of visiting the temple, I will rather go and see the town, which lies beyond under the shroud of trees. It is some distance away, this buried city. Whereas there are scarcely ten yards between my upraised dwelling and the steps leading to the first galleries of the Sanctuary ; and it will be an easy thing to visit it at any time, let it rain how it may.

With the same creaking of wheels, the same rocking leisureliness, we cross again the park-like enclosure, passing through the gateway of the threshold and over the bridge where watch, like sentinels, the great serpents with their seven heads.

And, following the vague pathways of the bush, we plunge again beneath the infinite covering of the forest. The heat, which weighs as heavily as ever upon our shoulders, becomes all at once shady and moist. Little vortices of mosquitoes envelop us, and we breathe that peculiar kind of malaria which induces the "fever of the woods."

We had been travelling for about an hour through the uninterrupted forest, amongst unfamiliar flowers, when the ramparts of the town at last rose before us, themselves wrapt in the deep green night of the forest, beneath the entanglement of branches. They were defended formerly by a moat measuring some hundred

yards across, which in the lapse of time has
been filled up by earth and dead leaves, so that
no trace of it remains; and they had a circumference of more than twelve miles. As we
come upon them now they look like rocks,
so high and blunted are they, so disrupted by
the patient labour of roots, so overgrown with
brambles and ferns. The " Gate of Victory,"
under which we are about to pass, might at
first sight be mistaken for the entrance to a
cavern overhung with creepers.

In epochs that are uncertain, this town, buried
now for many centuries, was one of the glories
of the world. Just as the old Nile, by virtue
merely of its slime, had reared in its valley a
marvellous civilization, so here the Mekong,
spreading each year its waters, had deposited a
richness, and prepared the way for the proud
empire of the Khmers. It was probably in the
time of Alexander the Macedonian, that a people,
emigrated from India, came and settled on the
banks of this great river, after subjugating the
timid natives—men with little eyes, worshippers
of the serpent. The conquerors brought with
them the gods of Brahmanism and the beautiful legends of the Ramayana; and as their
opulence increased on this fertile soil, they

built everywhere gigantic temples, carved with a thousand figures.

Later—some centuries later, one cannot well say how many, for the existence of this people is much effaced from the memory of man—the powerful sovereigns of Angkor saw, arriving from the East, missionaries in yellow robes, bearers of the new light at which the Asiatic world was wondering. Buddha, the predecessor of his brother Jesus, had achieved the enlightenment of India, and his emissaries were spreading over the east of Asia, to preach there that same gospel of pity and love which the disciples of Christ had recently brought to Europe. Then the savage temples of Brahma became Buddhist temples; the statues of the altars changed their attitudes and lowered their eyes with gentler smiles.

It would seem that under Buddhism the town of Angkor knew the apogee of its glory. But the history of its swift and mysterious decline has never been written, and the invading forest guards the secret of it. The little Cambodia of to-day, the repository and preserver of complicated rites of which the significance is no longer known, is a last remnant of that vast empire of the Khmers, which for more than

THE GATE OF VICTORY, ANGKOR-THOM

five hundred years now has been buried under the silence of trees and weeds.

Through the gloom then we approach the "Gate of Victory," which at first seemed to us the entrance of a cave. It is surmounted, nevertheless, with monstrous representations of Brahma, which are hidden from us by the entwined branches, and on either side, in a kind of niche overhung by foliage, shapeless triple-headed elephants wait as if in ambush.

Beyond this gate crowned with gloomy visages, we penetrate into what was once the immense town. It is well that one should be advised of it, for, within the walls, the forest continues, as deep in shade, as serried as without, and the age-old branches bate nothing of their height. We descend from our carts at this point and advance on foot by pathways that are scarcely discernible, tracks, as they might be, of wild beasts. For guide I have my Cambodian interpreter who is a familiar of the ruins; and as I follow him the sound of our footsteps is smothered in the herbage, and we hear only the quiet gliding of the snakes, the nimble flight of the monkeys.

Scarcely recognisable débris of architecture may be seen, however, on every side, mingled with and almost concealed by ferns and cycads and orchids, by all that flora of the eternal twilight which flourishes here beneath the vault of the high trees. A number of Buddhist idols, some small, some of medium size, and some giantlike, seated on thrones are smiling at nothing. They had been carved out of hard stone, and have remained, each in its place, after the downfall of the temples, which it would seem must have been made of sculptured wood. In almost every case pious pilgrims have made for them a roof of thatch as a shelter from the heavy storm showers; some one has even burnt sticks of incense to them, and brought them flowers. But no monks dwell in their neighbourhood on account of the dreaded "fever of the woods," which makes it dangerous to sleep under the thickness of the green tufts, and even at the times of the great pilgrimages they are left to pass their nights in solitude.

Here once were palaces; here lived kings in all the glory of their prodigious pride, of whom we now know nothing, who have passed into oblivion without leaving so much as a name graven on a stone or in a memory. They have been built by men, these towering rocks, which are now made one with the forest, entwined and crushed by thousands of roots, as in the tentacles of an octopus.

For there is a passion for destruction even amongst the plants. The Prince of Death, called by the Brahmans Shiva, he who for each kind of animal has created the particular enemy which destroys it, for every creature its devouring worm, seems to have foreseen in the very night of the beginning of the world, that men would try to perpetuate themselves a little by building things that might endure. And so, to annihilate their work, he conceived, amongst a thousand other agents of destruction, the species of plant known as the parietary, and, chief of all, the "fig-tree of ruins" which nothing is able to withstand.

The "fig-tree of ruins" reigns to-day as undisputed master over Angkor. Above the palaces, above the temples, which it has patiently disintegrated, it flaunts everywhere in triumph its pale, sleek branches, spotted like a snake, and its large dome of leaves. At the beginning it was only a small grain, sown by the wind on a frieze or on the summit of a tower. But no sooner did it germinate than its roots, like tenuous filaments, insinuated their way between the stones, and proceeded to descend, descend, guided by a sure instinct, towards the earth. And when, at last, they reached the earth, they quickly swelled, waxing on the nourishing juices, until they became enormous, disjoining, displacing everything, cleaving from top to bottom the thick walls; and then the building was irretrievably lost.

The forest, always the forest, and always its shadow, its sovereign oppression. One feels instinctively that it is hostile, murderous, that it breeds fever and death; and at last one is seized with a desire to escape from it—it seems to imprison—it is terrifying. And then, suddenly, the rare birds that were singing become silent; and, suddenly, too, we are aware of a deeper obscurity. And yet the hour is not late. There must be something more than the thickness of the overhanging verdure to make the pathways seem so dark. A general drumming on the leaves announces the advent of a tropical deluge. We had not seen that, above the trees, the sky had suddenly become black. The water streams, pours in torrents upon our heads. Quickly, let us take refuge over there, near to that large, contemplative Buddha, in the shelter of his roof of thatch.

Siam

The involuntary hospitality of the god lasts for a considerable time, and there is in it something inexpressibly mournful in the mystery of the forest twilight, at the fading of the day.

When, at length, the deluge abates, it is time to take our departure if we wish to avoid being overtaken by the night in the forest. But we have almost reached Bayon, the most ancient of the sanctuaries of Angkor, celebrated for its quadruple - visaged towers. Through the semi-obscurity of the forest trees we can see it from where we stand, looking like a chaotic heap of rocks. We decide to take the risk and go to see it.

Through an inextricable tangle of dripping brambles and creepers, we have to beat our way with sticks in order to reach the temple. The forest entwines it strictly on every side, chokes it, crushes it; and to complete the destruction, immense "fig-trees" are installed there everywhere, up to the very summit of its towers, which serve them as a kind of pedestal. Here are the doors; roots, like aged beards, drape them with a thousand fringes; at this hour when it is already growing late, in the obscurity which descends from the trees and the rain-charged sky, they are deep, dark holes, which give one pause. From the first entrance that we reach, some monkeys which had come there for shelter, and were sitting in circle as if for some council, make their escape, without haste and without cry; it seems that in this place silence is imposed upon everything. We hear only the furtive sound of the water as it drips from the trees and stones after the storm.

My Cambodian guide is insistent that we should depart. We have no lanterns, he tells me, on our carts, and it behoves us to return before the hour of the tiger. So be it, let us go. But we make up our mind to return, expressly to visit this temple so infinitely mysterious.

Before I leave, however, I raise my eyes to look at the towers which overhang me, drowned in verdure, and I shudder suddenly with an indefinable fear as I perceive, falling upon me from above, a huge, fixed smile; and then another smile again, beyond, on another stretch of wall, . . . and then three, and then five, and then ten. They appear everywhere, and I realise that I have been overlooked from all sides by the faces of the quadrupled-visaged towers. I had forgotten them, although I had

Siam

been advised of their existence. They are of a size, these masks carved in the air, so far exceeding human proportions that it requires a moment or two fully to comprehend them. They smile under their great flat noses, and half close their eyelids, with an indescribable air of senile femininity, looking like aged dames discreetly sly. They are likenesses of the gods worshipped, in times obliterated, by those men whose history is now unknown; likenesses from which, in the lapse of centuries, neither the slow travail of the forest nor the heavy dissolving rains have been able to remove the *expression*, the ironical good humour, which is somehow more disquieting than the rictus of the monsters of China.

Our oxen trot smartly on the return journey, as if they, too, realised that it was necessary to escape before nightfall from this soaked and steaming forest, which now becomes dark almost suddenly, without any interval of twilight. And the memory of those over-large old dames, who are smiling yonder behind us, secretive above the heaps of ruins, continues to pursue me throughout the course of our jolting, rocking flight through the bush.

Siam

When at length I reach the open air again, before the large pools of water-lilies at the entrance to the cyclops bridge, the clear-swept sky has assumed a crystal-like clearness, and it is the hour when the stars begin to scintillate. At the further end of the glade, which now reappears, the towers of the temple of Angkor-Vat rise up very high. They are no longer, as at midday, pale and almost nebulous from the excess of sunlight; they stand out now with vivid clearness, outlining with the sharpness of a punching machine, against the background of greenish gold, the silhouettes of their elaborately wrought tiaras; and a large star, one of the first to be enkindled, shines above, magnificently. Then there comes back to me, like a refrain, the childish phrase of long ago : " In the depths of the forests of Siam, I have seen the star of evening rise over the ruins of Angkor."

After the stifling of the vaults of trees, after the forest full of ambushes, one gets at once a feeling of security, a sense of being at home, in returning to the immense enclosure of the temple, where the bushes are scarcely taller than a man, and the paved causeway goes straight and sure towards a semblance of a village. The chanting of the monks is also

THE CAUSEWAY, ANGKOR-VAT

there to welcome me, and when I climb by the
little ladder into my dwelling, built on piles
and without walls as it is, all seems hospitable
and good to me.

It is in the dead of night, preceded by a
Siamese torch-bearer, that I cross at last the
threshold of the colossal temple of Angkor-
Vat. It had been my original intention not to
begin the pilgrimage before to-morrow at daybreak; but I was tempted by the proximity
of the temple, the stupendous mass of which
seemed almost to overhang my frail lodging.

Mounting a flight of granite steps we reach
a gallery of prodigious length, which has the
intimidating sonority, and seemed at first to
have the silence of a cave; but no sooner do
we enter than it is filled at once with a multitudinous sound of rustling.

This is the exterior gallery, which forms a
square, of a side some two hundred and fifty
yards long, and surrounds, like a sumptuous
outer corridor, the staged entanglement of the
central buildings. Its flagstones are carpeted
with a nameless soft substance which yields to
our footsteps, shedding a mingled odour of
musk and dung. And to the rustling which

greeted our arrival are now added little piercing cries, which spread before us into the obscure distances.

As we pass our torch reveals to us, on the dark grey walls, an inextricable medley of warriors gesticulating furiously; along the whole length of the gallery, an uninterrupted bas-relief stretches out of sight its tale of battles, of combatants in thousands, of caparisoned elephants, of monsters, of war - chariots. . . . I have no intention of venturing to - night into the dangerous labyrinth of the centre, into the temple properly so-called, but I should like to make the circuit of the outer galleries, which are so straight and look so easy, and to continue to follow to the end the unrolling of the bas-relief. But I am troubled by these little piercing cries above my head, which are multiplied in concert, as if uttered by thousands of rats. . . . And then, high up, where one would look to see the stones of the vault, does it not seem that there is a quivering of black substances? . . . Oh! the adorable creatures carved here and there upon the walls, as if to afford a respite to the eyes from the long battle: holding in their hand a lotus flower, they stand two by two, or three by three, calm and smiling

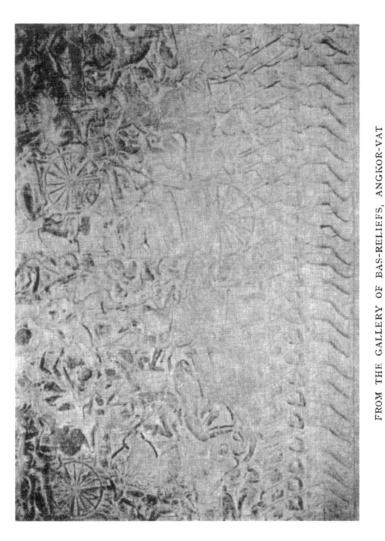

FROM THE GALLERY OF BAS-RELIEFS, ANGKOR-VAT

beneath their archaic tiaras. They are the divine Apsaras of the Hindoo theogonies. How lovingly the artists of old have chiselled and polished their Virgin-like breasts! . . . What has become, I wonder, of the dust of the beauties from whom their perfect bodies were copied? . . . Horror! the vault here sinks towards us, or at least the quivering black stuffs which seem to be suspended from it. . . . They descend so as to touch our hair; we can feel the wind they make like a vigorous fanning. . . . Hairy bodies moving very rapidly long hairless wings. . . . It was these, then, that uttered those cries above, like so many rats. . . . We are beset from all sides . . . enormous bats, in a cloud, in an avalanche, maddened, aggressive, . . . they threaten to extinguish our little mockery of a light. Quick, let us escape, make for the doors; this temple obviously ought not to be profaned in the solemn hours of the night.

Outside, sudden peace, serenity of sky, and splendour of stars. We arrest the course of our flight to inhale deliciously; the air is fragrant with jasmine, and the tranquil psalmody of the monks, after those multitudinous cries, seems an exquisite music. All those tortured figures which peopled the walls, and all those contacts of horrible wings. . . . Ugh! from what hideous nightmare have we escaped?

It is the enchanted hour of these regions, the hour when the brazier of the sun is extinguished, and the evil dew has not begun to shed its moisture. In the immense glade, defended by moats and walls, in the middle of which the temple is throned, one has a feeling of complete security, notwithstanding the surroundings and the proximity of the great forests. The tigers do not cross the bridges of stone, although now the gates are never shut, and, save for some curious monkeys, the beasts of the forests respect the enclosed park where men dwell and sing.

And the long causeway is there, stretching before me, whitish in the night, between the dark tufts of the bushes scented with jasmine and tuberose. Without aim, I begin to wander slowly over its flagstones, getting further and further away from the temple, hearing less and less distinctly the song of the monks, which by degrees dies away behind me into the infinite silence.

I wander on and on until I reach the water-lilied moat, with its bridge guarded by the seven - headed serpents. On the further bank the forest spreads its high black curtain; it draws me to it, with its air of sleep and mystery. Without entering it, what if I went just so far as the edge of its tall trees, surcharged now with night, where so many sleepless ears must already have heard me. And cautiously I pass through the portico, making sure of each stone upon which, gropingly, I set my foot; in such darkness as this, the bridge is formidable to cross.

But I seem to hear light footsteps running towards me from behind. Are they men or monkeys? And before I have time to turn round I feel myself taken by the hand, but without any sort of roughness, and two human shapes appear, who seek to detain me. I recognise them at once—they are two of my worthy Siamese ox-drivers. What do they want with me? To understand one another we have no single word of any language in common. But they make clear to me by signs that it is foolhardy to proceed further; there are ambushes yonder, and there are beasts with teeth that bite. And I let them have their way and lead me back.

They bring me to a corner of election, where

some other ox-drivers, also of my company, are stretched smoking cigarettes in the enjoyment of the cool air. It is on the wide, low rampart wall, which forms a kind of terrace above the defending moat. It seems that I am expected to lie down too. To do so on the earth itself would be impossible on account of the numerous sly, poisonous things which crawl in the grass; but on the old polished flagstones there is no sort of risk. One of the drivers takes off the thin tunic which covered his copper-coloured body, and, rolling it into a ball, makes a pillow for my head; after which I must needs smoke one of their cigarettes which exhales a strangely pleasant and soothing odour of burning herb. We know not how to talk to one another, but —no doubt because silence here has in it something intimidating—one of the young drivers intones very softly in falsetto a little lullaby which sounds like the lament of some spirit of the ruins; merely to hear it makes me feel that I have wandered far, into a country at once unknown and incomprehensible. And the constellations, too, which above my upturned head shine in the blue black of the infinite, make to me in their own way a permanent signal of exile. The Great Bear, which is throned on high in our nights of France, seems to have slipped down the sky; it has almost disappeared below the horizon; while, on the opposite side, I see shining, very significantly, the Southern Cross.

It is at first a delicious sensation to recline thus, half-naked, confident of the equable and caressing warmth of an atmosphere which never at any time grows chill, in which one knows that there will never rise a breeze that is not gentle. But the moments of well-being in these regions are numbered; around us a slight humming sound, faint to begin with, swells minute by minute, and becomes general: the mosquitoes are assembling, having scented from a distance the unwonted odour of flesh. And already, too, the linen with which I am clothed begins to soften and grow damp. The eternal moisture of these regions, which had made truce for an hour or two, reappears now in the form of dew. We are powdered, as it were, with tiny drops of water, and it behoves us to seek shelter at the foot of the temple, in the village of the chanting monks, beneath the hangar of the pilgrims.

It is under this hangar, protected by its little altar to Buddha, that I prepare at last to sleep. The piles upraise me from the ground where poisonous beasts crawl, and an outspread curtain of muslin is my protection against the beasts that prey. Around me the yellow ox-drivers of my train instal themselves, and, as they have no mosquito nets, they arrange to take turns until the morning in maintaining, beneath the open-work flooring of our lodging, a large fire of herbs, which will envelop us all in a protecting cloud. And, lulled by the Buddhist chant, I soon fall into a deep sleep, in the midst of an odorous smoke.

CHAPTER VIII

CHAPTER VIII

I AM awakened at dawn by the matinal crescendo of the psalmodies. There has been such an excess of humidity during the night, so heavy a dew, that in spite of the thatched roof everything around me and on me is soaked, as after a shower.

In the comparative freshness of the early morning, I climb again the first steps of the temple, between the worn balustrades, defaced by the rains of centuries. And, mindful of the guardian bats, I enter with an excess of caution, making no more noise than a cat. My enemies of last night are all asleep above, hanging, head downwards, by their claws to the stones of the ceiling, and simulating at this hour myriads of little bags of dark-coloured velvet. I have entered now, and none of them has so much as moved. I recognise the gallery, with its resonance as of a cave, which is decorated, as far as eye can see, with the endless bas-relief of battles. And now that I see it in its entirety, diminishing before me in unbroken perspective, it seems even more infinitely long than before. A green half light has replaced all at once the clear daylight that was broadening outside. There is a smell of dampness, such as one meets in subterranean places, but it is dominated here by the fusty musk-scented odour of the excrement of the bats, which is deposited in a layer upon the ground as if a rain of brown grains fell constantly from the vault.

To illumine the unfolding of the bas-relief, which covers all the interior wall of the gallery, windows at intervals open on to the surrounding park, and admit an attenuated light, made green by the foliage and palms. Very sumptuous windows, too, framed with carvings so delicate that one might think lace had been overlaid on the stone. They have annulated bars, which look like little columns of wood, elaborately turned by lathe, but are, in fact, of sandstone, like the rest of the walls.

This bas-relief, which stretches its medley of personages for more than a thousand yards, on the four sides of the temple, is inspired by one of the most ancient epics conceived by the

CARVINGS FROM ANGKOR-VAT

men of Asia — those Aryans who were our
ancestors.

"Formerly, in the age called Kuta, lived
the sons of Kyacyapa, who were of superhuman
strength and beauty. They had been born
of two sisters, Diti and Aditi. But the sons
of Aditi were gods, while the sons of Diti
were demons.

"One day when they were all assembled in
council to discover a means by which they
might escape old age and death, they decided
to gather all those plants of the woods which
are called simples, to cast them into the ocean,
and then to churn the ocean. There would
result from this a magic beverage which would
conquer death and make them strong and
beautiful for ever.

"Accordingly they made a churn with a
mountain, and a cord with the great holy
serpent Vasuki, and set themselves to churn
unceasingly.

"Presently, from the swirling waters, arose
the Apsaras, celestial dancers and courtesans,
who were of a beauty beyond compare. The
Gandharwas, the demi-gods, took them to wife,
and they gave birth to the race of monkeys.

"Then there appeared in person the beautiful
Varuni, daughter of the Ocean, whom the sons
of Aditi espoused. And finally, on the surface

of the waters, they saw forming the marvellous liquor which was to triumph over death. But for its possession a war of extermination began between the sons of Diti and the sons of Aditi, and the sons of Aditi conquered."

Such in brief summary is the theme of the Ramayana, that ancestral legend which has come down to us thanks to the labours of the pious Valmiki, who in the night of time, took pains to transcribe and perpetuate it in a poem of twenty-five thousand verses.

The churning of the ocean alone fills a panel more than fifty yards long. Then come the battles of the gods and demons, and those of the monkeys against the evil spirits of the Isle of Ceylon, who had ravished the beautiful Sita, the spouse of Rama.

All these pictures, which formerly were painted and gilded, have taken on, under the oozings of the eternal dampness, a mournful blackish colour, varied in places by glistenings of actual wetness. And, moreover, the bas-relief, which measures some sixteen feet in height, is worn, as high as a man can reach, by the secular friction of fingers—for in the times of pilgrimage the whole multitude makes it a duty to touch it. Here and there, in the parts illumined by the beautiful windows with their wreathed bars, one can still see traces of colouring on the robes and faces; and sometimes in the tiaras of the Apsaras, a little gold, spared by time, continues to shine. As I advance I do not cease to watch the velvet guardians above; the flagstones give out a hollow sound, and when my footsteps make too great a noise, some pairs of hairless wings are unfolded; a bat stretches itself, wakes another one, and a general stirring ensues. Then I stand quite still, as if turned to stone, until all are asleep again.

What is difficult to understand is that the wall with its multitude of figures seems to be in a single piece over a length of some hundreds of yards; it needs a close scrutiny to detect the joints of the enormous stones which have been placed together in line without the help of any cement, and adjusted with the same rigorous precision as in the monuments of Egyptian antiquity.

In the middle of each side of the quadrilateral, a portico opens from this outer gallery and gives access to the central court, where rises the pagoda properly so-called, the prodigious mass of sculptured stone scaling the blue sky. Into that I hesitate to penetrate, intimidated, perhaps, or wearied in advance by such an entanglement of stairways, terraces, and towers, by such a complication of lines, by the unspeakable grimness which characterises the silent whole. Rather than enter, I continue to loiter, following the bas-relief of the outer wall.

In the gallery on the fourth side I encounter two young monks — clothed in lemon - yellow robes beneath orange yellow draperies. What are they doing here with a wheel-barrow, a shovel, and a broom? Nothing more nor less than gathering the dung of the bats to manure some little monachal garden. I wonder how many thousands of millions of insects, eaten in the air, are represented by these heaps of brown grains in their barrow, which are on the way now to fertilise flowers, which will nourish other insects, which will be eaten by other bats!

But they are making too much noise, these young monks — although in truth they make scarcely any—for, above, the velvety sleepers are awakening.

To avoid their hairless wings, I rush hastily through one of the porticoes into the central courtyard. And thus, after having lingered for a long time around the wooded chaos of the sanctuaries, I enter at last with precipitation, in an impulse of flight.

It is at a moment when the light all at once becomes overcast, as if the sun were passing through some great eclipse. Above the masses of terraces, of porticoes and stairways, entangled with prodigal verdure, the clouds have suddenly spread a canopy of darkness; a diluvial rain is about to pour upon the ruins. And all the beasts which dwell there under the trees and in the breaches of the walls become silent, attentive to that which is about to fall.

This temple is one of the places in the world where men have heaped together the greatest mass of stones, where they have accumulated the greatest wealth of sculptures, of ornaments, of foliage, of flowers, and of faces. It is not simple as are the lines of Thebes and Baalbeck. Its complexity is as bewildering even as its enormity. Monsters guard all the flights of steps, all the entrances; the divine Apsaras, in indefinitely repeated groups, are revealed everywhere amongst the overhanging creepers. And, at a first view, nothing stands out; there seem only disorder and confusion in this hill of carved stones, on the summit of which the great towers have sprouted.

Siam

But, on the contrary, when one examines it a little, a perfect symmetry is manifest from top to base. The hill of sculptured stones forms a square pyramid of three stages, the base of which measures more than a thousand yards in circumference; and it is on the third and highest of these stages that we shall find, no doubt, that which is pre-eminently the holy place. We have to climb, therefore—I was prepared for it— to climb by steep and uneven steps, between the smiling Apsaras, the crouching lions, the holy serpents spreading like a fan their seven heads, and the languid verdure, which at this moment is motionless in the still air; to climb in haste, too, so as to reach the top before the deluge begins. In coming here this morning, I had imagined that the ascent would be made under a blue sky and in the glare of the sun; that the branches would be astir with gentle breezes, and that around me I should hear the sounds of birds, insects, and reptiles as they fled at my approach. But this mournful stillness daunts me; I was not prepared for this silence of waiting or for this black sky. My arrival wakens not a single sound, not a single move- ment, and even the sing-song of the monks, as they chant without ceasing at the foot of the temple, reaches me only very faintly, from the distance.

And now I have reached the first of the three platforms. Before me rises the second stage, of a height double that of the first, presenting stairways more abrupt, more guarded by smiles and rictus of stone. It is surrounded on its four sides by a vaulted gallery, a kind of cloister, immense and pompously magnificent, with its excess of carvings, its porticoes crowned with strange, elaborate frontals, with its narrow windows, the stone bars of which, already too massive, are brought close together as if the better to imprison you. All around the dilapidation is extreme. Within, the decoration is simpler than in the corridors of the base. The place is damp and dark, and there is an almost intolerable odour of bats; they cover the vault, these suspended sleepers. . . . At this height I no longer hear anything of the litany of the monks, and the silence is so profound that one scarcely dares to walk.

The second platform is surrounded like the first by a cloister, the façades of which are wrought with as much elaboration as the most patient embroideries. Here one might reasonably think that he was nearly there; but now

the third stage rises, of a height double that of
the second, and the monumental stairway that
leads up to it, with its worn, grass-grown steps,
is so steep that it induces a sensation of vertigo,
The gods desire, no doubt, to make themselves
more inaccessible in proportion as one endeavours
to approach them. And verily the temple
seems to grow higher, to stretch out, to reach
up towards the darkling sky, and it is a little
like those baffling dreams in which we strive
madly to reach a goal which flies before us . . .
There should be four of these staircases, watched
over by smiling Apsaras, one on each of the
sides of the enormous pedestal ; but I have not
time to choose the best, for the shadow of
the clouds grows ever deeper, and the storm
is at hand. I mount, almost running, and the
forest, the sovereign forest, seems to rise at the
same time ; on every side it begins to stretch
its circle to the horizon like a sea.

Here now is the third square platform,
bordered also with its cloister, the façades of
which are carved even more magnificently still.
In high relief on the walls are the inevitable
Apsaras standing in groups, and welcoming me
with smiles of quiet mockery, the eyes half-
closed. On this, the highest of the terraces,

A WINDOW, ANGKOR-VAT

Siam

where I reach the bases of the towers, and the very doors of the sanctuary, I must be about a hundred feet above the level of the plains. And here the illusion is reversed. It seems now that it is the temple which has sunk into the forest. Seen from here it looks to be submerged, buried up to its middle in verdure. Below me, three graduated courses of cloisters, of high-crowned porticoes, of sumptuous vaults, scarcely broken by the centuries, have plunged, as it were, into the trees, into the silent expanse of trees, the tufts of which, in the distance, and as far as eye can see, simulate the undulations of an ocean swell.

The rain! A few first drops, astonishingly large and heavy, by way of warning. And then almost at once the general drumming on the leaves, torrents of water which descend with fury. Then, through a portico, the over-loaded frontal of which is in the form of flames and horns, running to take shelter, I enter at least what must be the sanctuary itself.

I expected an immense hall, where I should be alone, whereas it is only another gallery infinitely long but narrow, oppressive, sinister— in which I shudder almost at meeting, in the half-light of the storm and the barred windows, a number of motionless people—people eaten by worms, corpses and phantoms of gods, seated and foundering along the walls.

The majority are of human stature, but some are giantlike, and others are dwarfs. Some are of a dull grey, others of blood-coloured red, and here and there a little gilding, as in the masks of the mummies, shines still on certain of the faces. Many are without hands, without arms, without head, and a mass of excrement, the offering of our friends the bats, humps their back, deforms their shoulders. And when I raise my eyes, how the sight fills me with disgust! For here, more even than below, the stone ceilings are tapestried with these little velvet pockets which hang suspended by their claws, and want but the slightest noise to unfold and become a whirlwind of wings. The interior of the thick, blackish walls, void of any kind of ornament, are half concealed by fine spun draperies, like funereal crapes, which are the work of innumerable spiders. Without, I hear the storm raging. Everything is inundated; the water streams in veritable cascades. I breathe a warm vapour at once fetid and musk-scented. In the long gallery the closeness of the walls and the enormous size of the sandstone columns which mask the openings induce a feeling of confinement ; and this, notwithstanding that the circle of the horizon, seen between the same window bars, supports the notion of altitude, serves as a reminder that one dominates, from the height of this kind of aerial prison, the infinite expanse of the sodden forest.

This, then, is the sanctuary which haunted many years ago my childish imagination. I reach it at last only after many journeyings about the world, in what is already the evening of my wandering life. It gives me mournful welcome. I had not foreseen these torrents of rain, this confinement amongst the webs of spiders, nor my present solitude in the midst of so many phantom gods. There is a personage beyond, conspicuous amongst them all, reddish in colour like a flayed corpse, with feet worm-eaten and crumbling, who, in order that he may not fall altogether, leans crosswise against the wall, half-upturning his face with its scarred lips. It is from him, it seems, that all the silence and all the unutterable sadness of the place proceed.

A prisoner here for so long as the storm may last, I go first of all to a window, instinctively, to get more air, to escape from the odour of the bats. And between the rigid spindle-shaped bars, I see sloping below me the architectural mass which I have just ascended. On the sides of the ruins, all the foliage bends and trembles, overwhelmed by the tumultuous downpour. The legions of Apsaras, the great holy serpents, the monsters crouching on the threshold of the flights of steps, seem to bow the head under the daily deluge, which, for seasons without number, has worn by dint of washing them. More and more I hear the water crackling, rushing in a thousand streams.

In order to discern the general plan of this third and highest platform, it would be necessary to see it from outside. But the light continues to diminish, as if it were the twilight instead of the morning; the horizon of the forests is completely hidden behind the opaque curtains of the rain, and it is clear that the storm will last for another hour at least. I have, perforce, to remain in shelter, and, in this persistent twilight of eclipse, feeling that I am followed by the cadaverous smiles of all this assembly of Buddhas, who are watching me, I proceed towards what must be the centre and very heart of Angkor-Vat.

AN ANGLE OF A COURT, ANGKOR-VAT

Siam

I tread softly on the layers of dust and excrement, sprinkled with feathers of owls. The huge, hairy spiders, weavers of the multiple draperies, remain motionless and on watch.

Over and above that which falls unceasingly from the roof, little heaps of withered flowers and incense appear before all the idols, attesting that men venerate them still. But why do not people dust them a little when they come to visit them? And in what disorder, too, they have been left!—the small, the large, and the colossal, all higgledy-piggledy as after a rout. At the uncertain date of the sack of the town and the pillage of the temple they were all overthrown and dragged to earth. Subsequently the piety of the Siamese put them upright again, as best it could, but in a methodless grouping along the walls, those of sandstone against those of worm-eaten wood, which crumble to powder at the slightest touch, those which have lost their colouring side by side with those which still possess red robes and gilded faces. (And, lest they should forget a single one of them in their devotions, the pilgrims who come hither spend hours, it seems, in passing through the endless galleries where they repose.) Buddhist statues, already

centenarian many times over, they were yet
new-comers, quite recent intruders in this
temple of a far more ancient cult. And having
supplanted the images of Brahma, the primitive
god of Angkor, they are now fallen in their
turn, destroyed by time.

The flagstones are so carpeted with filth
and ashes that the sound of my footsteps is
smothered, and, without being heard by the
thousands of little ears above, I make my way
towards the darker end of the gallery, between
the two rows of silent personages. Here,
formerly, was the Holy of Holies, the place
where the supreme Brahma was enthroned;
but it has been walled up for an unknown
period of time.

And before this wall—which, no doubt, still
encloses the terrible idol, and perhaps preserves
it as intact as a mummy in its sarcophagus
—a Buddha of gigantic size, commanding and
gentle, has been seated for centuries, with legs
crossed and downcast half-closed eyes, for so
many centuries that the spiders have contrived
patiently to drape him with black muslins,
hiding the gold with which he is adorned, and
that the bats have had time to cover him as
with a thick mantle. The swarm of horrible

little sleeping beasts forms now a kind of padded daïs of brown plush above his head, and the rain, which continues to stream mercilessly outside, makes for him its plaintive daily music. But his bowed head, which I can distinguish in spite of the darkness, preserves the same smile as may be found on all representations of Him, from Thibet to China: the smile of the Great Peace, obtained by the Great Renunciation and the Great Pity.

This evening, as I once more ascend to the temple, after having slept below, at its foot, in the hangar of the pilgrims, during the heat of the day, this evening one would never believe that it had rained in torrents all the morning. In the sky is a blue splendour that seems immutable. The earth has quickly drunk up the superabundant water, and the burning sun has dried the trees of the forest and the verdure which encroaches upon the ruins. All is luminous, calm, and hot, much more so than in the finest of our summer days. The Apsaras, the monsters, the half-effaced bas-reliefs, the masses of immense dead stones, are bathed now in a sort of ironical and mournful magnificence. And the thousands of little invaders of the sanctuary, those which fly, those which run, and those which crawl, have emerged from their hiding-places of the morning, and begun again their insatiate hunt for provender. All around I hear the rustling of serpents and lizards, the singing of turtle-doves and little birds, the meowing of wild cats. Large butterflies, like figurings of precious silks, career about, and myriads of flies, in corselets of velvet and golden green, mingle with the psalmody of the monks a murmur like the distant pealing of bells. The bats alone, the inevitable bats, prime masters of Angkor-Vat, sleep on in their perpetual shadow, glued to the vaults of the cloisters.

With time and neglect each of the superposed terraces of the temple has become a kind of suspended garden where the immense leaves of the banana palms are mingled with the white tufts of a most fragrant jasmine clustered with blossom. All this, and a thousand other exotic plants and the tall wanton herbage—all this, after seeming to die beneath the whipping of the rain, has risen again more vigorous than before, and with a freshness more sparkling amidst the decrepitude of the stones.

Without hurrying this time, for no cloud threatens me, I climb the arduous steps which lead, above, to the dwelling of the gods. Oh, the graceful and exquisite carvings scattered in profusion everywhere! These scrolls, these traceries of leaf and flower—how inexplicable it seems—resemble those which appeared in France in the time of Francis I. and the Medicis. For a moment one might be tempted to believe, if it were not an impossibility, that the artists of our Renascence had sought their models on these walls, which, nevertheless, in their days had been slumbering for three or four centuries, in the midst of forests, quite unsuspected by Europe.

I climb without haste, lighted by a sun of dazzlement and death, and along my laborious ascending route is marshalled an endless array of intimidating symbols. Everywhere monsters, and combats of monsters. Everywhere the sacred Naga, trailing over the balustrades its long, undulating body, and then rearing like a scarecrow its seven viperish heads. The Apsaras, how pretty and smiling they are, in their coiffures of goddesses, with, nevertheless, always that expression of reserve and mystery which is so little reassuring. Richly adorned, with bracelets, necklaces, headbands of precious stones, tall tiaras, either pointed or surmounted with a tuft of plumes, they hold between their delicate fingers sometimes a lotus flower, and sometimes an enigmatic emblem. And all of them that one can reach in passing have been so often caressed in the course of centuries, that their beautiful bare bosoms shine as under a varnish. For the women, who come hither during the pilgrimages, touch them passionately in order that they may obtain from them the grace to become mothers. In their niches embroidered with carvings, they remain adorable. But what a pity that their feet should so disfigure them! They are always enormous as in the bas-reliefs of Egypt, and always drawn in profile, whilst the legs face you fully. And yet there is cause for reflection, too, in these ineptly drawn feet, for they remind us that the fair goddesses are the work of a very primitive humanity, which in its art was still battling with the difficulties of draughtsmanship, still baffled by the mystery of foreshortening.

And there is another thing of which they were ignorant, those proud architects of Angkor-Vat, and that is the wide expanded vault. Their ancestors had taught them only that which is obtained by corbelling, and must perforce remain narrow and heavy. That is why all the galleries

A DOOR-POST, ANGKOR-VAT

they contrived to build are suffocating, why they superposed cloisters and cloisters, staged massive terraces on massive terraces, heaped blocks on the top of blocks. And this temple, no doubt, with that of Bayon, foundered in the neighbouring forest, is the mightiest piling of stones that men have dared to undertake since the pyramids of Memphis.

As each stage is reached, there is a momentary respite of shade, in the hot dampness of the bordering cloister.

But a sun of fire glares on the last staircase, which is twice as high as the preceding one, and the steepest of all, the staircase which leads to the topmost platform and seems to climb into the sky. And, truly, this progressive doubling of the height, from one stage to another, is a notable architectural discovery for increasing the size of the temple by an illusion from which it is difficult to escape. I experience it this evening as I experienced it this morning under the dark rain-clouds : it is as if the dwelling of the gods, in measure as you approach it, flies before you, soaring into the air.

It is designed, too, and in a very effective way religious, this successive diminution of the internal decoration, the nearer one approaches the Holy of Holies. I had already remarked the employment of similar means in the Brahmanistic temples of India, more particularly in those of Ellora, where after a surfeit of sculpture in the lower galleries, the supreme symbol is found at last at the bottom of a savage hall with thick bare walls : the idea being that the place where the divine symbol dwells should contain nothing that might distract the visitors from worship and awe.

Arriving again in the last of the successive terraces, I enter a gallery of phantom idols, similar to that in which I took refuge during the storm, which leads in the darkness to a door sealed with stones, and before this door, also, a large Buddha, very gentle in aspect, is seated as watchman. But this is not the same gallery as I was in this morning. I do not recognise the scarred faces of the personages who inhabit it, and, besides, I have come to it by different staircases, different porticoes.

It is now about five o'clock, and the golden rays of the sun are tinged a little with the red of the evening. There is no slightest trace of the deluge of the morning. I am able now to report that, on this platform of the summit, there are four identical galleries, equally

long, equally populous with funereal hosts, hung
with the same black spider webs, and wadded
on the ceiling with the same sleeping bats.
These four galleries make a cross with equal
arms and converge upon the Holy of Holies,
which marks the centre of the mountain-temple.
But, after the extreme prodigality of ornamentation in the cloisters below, these highest naves,
richly embellished as they are without, disclose,
in the interior, only square rough-hewn pillars
and rugged and defaced walls. It is the sign that
one should enter here only for prayer, having
freed the spirit from all the false shows of the
world. They were the thresholds of the
Invisible and the Inexpressible, and it needed
there nothing that might recall our vanities,
our earthly luxuries. And in their dark
depths, behind the identical giant Buddhas,
their identical doors, which to-day are sealed,
are closed upon the four faces of the supreme
retreat—where, perhaps, the soul of the old
temple subsists still, buried with the terrible
Brahmas.

One of those colossal towers, in outline like
tiaras, which can be seen so far away in the
plain, rises at the end of each arm of the
cross formed by the four naves, and, above

the Holy of Holies where the naves meet, a
fifth tower, the most wonderful and the most
elaborate, surpassing all the others, commands,
from a height of more than two hundred feet,
the thick, green shroud of the forest. Accord-
ing to a learned Chinese writer, who visited this
mysterious empire on the eve of its decline,
about the thirteenth century, and has left us
the only known documents concerning its
magnificence, this central tower was crowned
with a golden lotus, so large that its sacred
flower could be seen shining in the air from
every point of the town, which to-day lies
buried.

In the forest which surrounds me, and is
revealed, under this pure evening sky, clear
and distinct to the circle of the horizon, I had
not noticed this morning a number of trees
of annual foliage, here and there, which are
turning yellow, and shedding their leaves,
because December is at hand. It reminds me
that in coming hither I have, in fact, journeyed
northwards for three or four days, and that
already the country is not absolutely one of
perpetual greenness, as was the Cochin-China
I have left. And in spite of the powerful,
tranquil heat, an unexpected impression of

THE CENTRAL TOWER, ANGKOR-VAT

autumn, of falling leaves, as in the forests of France, comes to augment for me all at once the nameless melancholy of these ruins.

I thought I should be alone to wander till nightfall in these high galleries. But, while I am watching, between the massive bars of a window, the sun, which before setting is turning everything to fire, some visitors, behind me, arrive with timid, velvety steps, old grey-bearded men. Their costumes proclaim them to be pilgrims from Burmah. Before each Buddha they make a salutation, deposit a flower, and light a stick of incense. Even to the most shapeless débris littering the floor, they pay a reverence, and whenever the remnant is in any way recognisable, an arm, a worm-eaten trunk, a head without a body, they stop and plant close by, between the joints of the pavement, one of their burning sticks. And thus once more the dead and musty air in which these images and these vestiges are achieving their return to dust is filled for a moment with a suave fragrance.

One of the pilgrims, however, the leader of the band, whispers something which seems to signify " Let us hasten, night is approaching, and would overtake us in the ruins."

Thereupon they curtail their devotions, their reverences become more hurried and less formal. Arrived before the Great Buddha, who, at the end of the gallery, guards the immured sanctuary, they select those places where the gilding of his legs is most faded, and carefully apply to them sheets of goldleaf which they extract from a portfolio. Then they depart. I hear the sound of their quiet footsteps die away as they descend the steep staircases of stone. Their departure has suddenly made the solitude more imposing, and seems to make the very daylight fade more quickly. Besides the setting of the sun is so vertical and so rapid in these regions, which are almost without twilight!

Below me, the darkness has already encroached upon the architectural mass of which I have now a bird's-eye view, and also upon the expanse of the surrounding forest, where presently will open, innumerable, the eyes of the nocturnal beasts. Alone, two towers, which rise up in my vicinity, are resplendent still, like glowing embers; the reddened rays light, as in apotheosis, their unknown architecture, which is neither Hindoo nor Chinese, which resembles that of no other country on the earth.

Siam

If the ornamentation of the walls, the scrolls, and foliage, recalled our European Renascence, these towers, on the contrary, are of a striking and utter strangeness — the conception of a race apart, which flashed a bright splendour in this corner of the world, and then disappeared to return no more. They resemble somewhat sheaves of organ-pipes, above which have been placed, at the various heights, richly ornamented crowns. The design is complicated, too, with Apsaras, with very strangely nimbused gods, with groups of monsters. In the sky, which is now changing and turning to the grey of twilight, they continue to glow for some seconds longer, looking like metal reddened by fire, like the burning towers of I know not what magic palace.

Formerly in place of this sea of verdure, silent at my feet, the town of Angkor-Thom (Angkor the Great) spread for some distance about the plain; and if we could now lop off the tufted branches we should see again, reappearing below, walls and terraces and temples; we should see, stretching away, long paved avenues bordered by how many divinities, seven-headed serpents, bell-turrets, balusters, all foundered now in the bush. But the deep forest has become again what it was from the beginning of the ages, for centuries beyond our power to calculate; there is now no outward sign of the work of those Hindoo adventurers, who, some three hundred years before our era, came and plied their axes here, clearing space for a town of nearly a million souls. No; it lasted for but fifteen hundred years, this episode of the Empire of the Khmers, for what might be called a mere negligible period, in comparison with the longevity of the reign of the vegetable world; and it is done with, the wound is healed, no trace of it remains. The fig-tree of ruins flaunts everywhere its dome of green leaves.

In our days, it is true, some new adventurers, come from a country nearer west (the country of France), are chafing in a small way the eternal forest, for they have founded not far from here a semblance of a little empire. But this latest episode will lack magnitude, and more especially it will lack duration. Soon, when these pale conquerors shall have left in turn, buried in this Indo-Chinese soil, many of their — alas, many poor young soldiers all guiltless of the mad adventure—they will pack their belongings and depart. Then there will

A COLONNADE, ANGKOR-VAT

be seen no more wandering in these regions, as I am wandering, men of the white race, who are so foolishly covetous of governing immemorial Asia, and of disturbing everything they find there.

The two fantastic, and, as they seemed, incandescent towers, which I was watching from this window, cool with singular rapidity— cool from their base, no doubt because the base is buried in the temple, which in turn is buried in the damp medley of trees. The red glow persists now only on the extreme point, and, as I watch, it changes quickly to violet and fades away.

The light of the immense panorama dies like the light of a lamp that is blown out, and the forest is filled with darkness beneath an ash-coloured sky, in which lingering green and yellow lights alone indicate the side where the sun has set. The Buddhas around me begin to cause me uneasiness. I imagine that they are playfully raising their shoulders under the thick brown mantles, which deform them so that they look like stout old dowagers swathed in fur.

The ruins are wrapt in a sudden majesty, and my continued presence seems a profanation.

Siam

And then a nameless horror issues from the darker recesses, where the befurred giants and hunch - backed dwarfs assume all at once the air of phantoms. It issues slowly, this insidious horror, trailing along the gallery like a sleepy wave towards the window where I was standing. I realise that it will fill the temple and that I cannot hope to escape it. It behoves me to depart, therefore, to descend in order that I may not be surprised by the darkness in the middle of the staircases, with their slippery steps overgrown with creepers. And, above my head, I can hear the little rat-like cries answering one another along the ceilings of resonant stone. It is the hour when all the hairless wings are about to unfold for the giddy dance about the old sanctuary, to resume the general whirl of every night, the great hunt, the great massacre of gnats and moths.

CHAPTER IX

CHAPTER IX

THERE has been another deluge during the
night lasting from two o'clock to four, and,
although the thatched roof has protected us
faithfully enough, the air is so impregnated
with moisture that we awake soaked as by the
storm itself.

Now, however, the day is broadening in a
pure splendour. The blue, cloudless sky is
innocence itself. I therefore have the oxen
harnessed to our little jogging carts, in
order to return to the forest and visit that
temple of Bayon, of which I had but a glimpse,
the day before yesterday, in the rainy twilight.

The sun has not long risen when we leave
the enclosed park and plunge at a trot beneath
the tall trees of the deep forest. At once a
green shade stretches over our heads and
around us rises a multitudinous music of birds
and insects delirious in the rapture of the

morning. Along the pathway, above the impenetrable thickets full of ferns, cycads and orchids, the trees rise to a prodigious height. Amongst them are some that have been scarred by men—so rare and stealthy as they are in these parts—who have notched them in order to collect, in earthen pots, I know not what precious essence. In the same manner one may see, in our country, the inhabitants of the Landes collect the resin of their pines. There are others of which the trunk, for about six feet above the ground, is all scratched, all furrowed with cruel rents. These are the trees used by the tigers, as obsessed in this respect as cats, to stretch their paws and sharpen their merciless claws, when they awaken in the evening after the long siesta of the day.

It is already becoming insufferably hot, with a moist unwholesome heat saturated with exhalations of the lush earth and wanton plants. In the rays of the sun which, here and there, traverse the foliage, we can see the insects in their endless whirligigs, and their little metallic-lustred bodies seem to throw off sparks of fire. The mosquitoes, those tiny carriers of fever, eddy everywhere in clouds of fine dust. Butterflies with bodies that are too light for their long silken wings, drift as they fly, seeming the plaything of the slightest breath, until they settle at last upon some singular pale-coloured flower of the shade. And the numberless birds which fly before us might be blue and red rockets thrown up in our passage through the semi-obscurity of the forest.

At the end of nearly an hour the crenellated wall of the tenebrous town of Angkor-Thom appears before us, without breaking the continuous vault of trees; and still in green night we descend from our ox-carts before the " Gate of Victory," above which, beneath a fringe of creepers, smiles a colossal human visage.

Having passed the ramparts, we continue to advance, but through a denser bush and by pathways less defined.

Half an hour's walk, about, in this forest sown with débris, which is the winding sheet of a town, where every stone bears trace of an antique sculpture, where the fragments one picks up in the grass represent a human mask. And then we reach a shapeless mass of rocks, a kind of mountain above which the fig-trees of ruins spread superbly their large green parasols. And this is Bayon. These rocks were builded long ago by the hand of man; they are factitious; they are the remains of one of the most prodigious temples of the world.

The destruction is bewildering. How could they come, these masses of stone, to warp thus, to bend, to fall, to be confounded in such chaos? There are towers which seem to have fallen in a single piece, to have descended in their entirety from their basements. And the massive terraces have broken. And all around the earth has mounted; the humus, in the course of centuries, has begun to climb the large staircases in its endeavour to swallow up the whole.

The immense faces of Brahma, "the gracious old ladies," so sly-looking and so little reassuring the other evening in the twilight, I see them again everywhere above my head, smiling upon me from between the ferns and roots. They are far more numerous than I thought. I can discern them even on the most distant of the towers, crowned and girt about the neck with necklaces. But in broad day, how they have lost their power to scare! They seem to say to me this morning: "We are quite dead, you see, and quite harmless. It is not out of irony we smile thus, with eyelids half-closed; it is

BAYON

because we have attained peace—peace without dreams."

The temple, of which the scarcely recognisable ruins are before me, represents the earliest conception, crude and savagely immense, of a people apart, without analogue in the world, and without neighbours: the Khmer people, a detached branch of the great Aryan race, which planted itself here as if by chance, and grew and developed far from the parent stem, separated from the rest of the world by immense expanses of forest and marshland. About the ninth century some four hundred years earlier than Angkor - Vat, this sanctuary, ruder and more enormous, was in the plenitude of its glory. In order to try and picture to one's self what was once its almost awful magnificence, it would be necessary, first of all, to clear away, in imagination, the forest which engulfs it, to suppress the inextricable entanglement of these roots and these greenish white-spotted branches, which are, so to say, the tentacles of the fig-tree of ruins; and then, no longer in this eternal green night, but in the open air, under the wide heaven, to re-erect these quadruple-visaged towers — about fifty towers! — to replace them upright on their monstrous pedestal, which like that of Angkor-Vat was in three stages. To imagine, afterwards, all around, a wide extent of open space so that men might see from afar the crushing stature of the whole; to re-construct the successive terraces, the steps, the sumptuous avenues which led hither, bordered by so many columns, balusters, divinities, and monsters, which to-day are foundered in the herbage.

These towers with their squat forms and superposed rows of crowns, might have been compared in outline to colossal pineapples placed on end. It was as if a vegetation of stone had sprouted in thick impetuous profusion from the soil; fifty towers of different heights rising in tiers; fifty fantastic pineapples, grouped in a kind of bundle on a base as large as a town, almost hugging one another and forming a retinue to a central and more gigantic tower, some two hundred feet in height, which dominated them, its summit crowned with a golden lotus-flower. And from high in the air, those quadruple faces with which each of them was adorned gazed at the four cardinal points, gazed everywhere, with the same drooping eyelids, the same expression of ironical pity, the same smile. They affirmed, they repeated until

Siam

it became a kind of obsession, the omnipresence of the god of Angkor. From whatever point of the immense town these aerial faces were always to be seen, some full - face, others in profile or three - quarter face, now gloomy under lowering rain-charged skies, now ardent, as with ruddy fire, at the setting of the sun, or, again, bluish and spectral on moonlit nights, but always there and always commanding. But to-day their reign is over; in the green twilight in which they are crumbling it is necessary, almost, to seek to find them, and the time is approaching when they will no longer be even recognisable.

To ornament the walls of Bayon, endless bas-reliefs and decorations of every sort have been conceived with an exuberant prodigality. Here, too, there are battles, furious conflicts, war-chariots, interminable processions of elephants, and groups of Apsaras, of Tevadas with pompous crowns. But under the moss everything is becoming effaced and perishing. The workman-ship is cruder and more naïve than at Angkor-Vat, but the inspiration revealed here is more vehement, more tumultuous. There is something disconcerting in so great a profusion. In our days of pinchbeck versatility it is difficult to realise the perseverance, the fertility, the faith, the love of the grand and eternal, which inspired this vanished people.

Beneath the central tower with its golden lotus, some sixty feet above the plain, was concealed the Holy of Holies, a dark retreat, stifling as a casemate in its thickness of stone. It was approached from many sides, by a veritable maze of converging galleries, as mournful as sepulchral chambers. But access to it to-day is difficult and dangerous, the approaches are so broken and ruinous. You feel that you are still beneath the forest—for the forest covers even the towers—beneath a multiple net-work of innumerable roots. It is very dark. A lukewarm water oozes from all the walls, on phantom gods without arms or without a head. You can hear the gliding of snakes, the flight of unascertained creeping beasts; and the bats awake, flicking you, by way of protest, with their rapidly moving wings which you have not seen coming. In Brahmanistic times this Holy of Holies was a place where men were wont to tremble, and centuries of neglect have not robbed it of its awe. It remains always the refuge of the ancient mysteries. The noises made by the furtive beasts as we entered cease

A DOORWAY, BAYON

as soon as we become still, and everything subsides at once into an intense silence, filled with I know not what horror of expectancy.

In this forest of shadow are to be found a number of other ruins, in disjointed and overthrown masses, beneath the beautiful, triumphant branches; débris of palaces, of temples, of piscinæ where men and elephants used to bathe. They bear witness still to the splendour of that empire of the Khmers, which flourished for fifteen hundred years unknown to Europe, and then perished after a swift decline, exhausted by a succession of wars with Siam, with Annam, and even with immemorial and stagnant China.

To my western eyes, the final impression received from these dead things is one of bafflement and mystery. The least stone, the least lintel over a portico, the least of these crownings imitating flames, is a cause of astonishment, like the revelation of a distant and hostile world. Monsters in greenish stone, seated in the attitude of dogs, and coifed in a fashion, doubtless, of some planet without communication with ours, welcome me with looks of startling strangeness, with rictus never previously seen, even in the old Chinese sanctuaries from which I come. "We do not know thee," they say to me. "We are conceptions for ever foreign to thee. What comest thou hither to do? Begone." And, moreover, as the sun ascends and blazes more fiercely above the vault of trees, an increasing heaviness retards our steps; as we walk we are more and more closely enveloped by a kind of aggressive dust, dancing and sparkling, which is a cloud of mosquitoes; and it is with a lassitude a little feverish that we continue to wander in this forest of dark enchantments. Enough! It is time to retrace our steps towards the "Gate of Victory," in order to return before midday to the enclosure of Angkor-Vat.

The burning hour is near when we again reach the shelter of the hangar of the pilgrims, where is heard from morning till evening, like an incantation, the psalmody of the yellow-robed monks.

And, after the mid-day repast, the irresistible tropical languor returns, as it returns every day, to prostrate us. It will be better to leave this hangar in which one stifles, and, braving the scorching of the sun, to cross the ten yards or so which separate me from the first galleries of the temple. In the shadow and perpetual dampness of the stone ceilings 1 may find at least an appearance of coolness. Let some one spread a mat there for me, after sweeping clear a space at a point where the vault is not too tapestried with bats, and I will sleep on the comparatively cool flagstones, covering my face with a fan as a protection from what may fall from the roof.

But, nevertheless, sleep is slow in coming to me, for I am lying at the very foot of the immense bas-relief of battles, and, spite of me, my heavy eyes are beguiled by it for a long time: silent torment; fury of great conflicts past and forgotten, slaughters sung by the poets of the Ramayana, but which no one any more remembers; confusion of muscular limbs, meeting in shock of battle between the army of the Giants and that of the King of the Monkeys, war-chariots crushing the wounded in hundreds. . . . In the prevailing gloom, all this, blackish and, as it were, varnished by the damp, is illumined in places by a glimmering half-light, and thus the reliefs are accentuated, a little life returns to the effaced rictus, to the dead contortions. I have lost the notion of the enormity of the neighbouring mass of architecture, but I feel that I have become intimate with those of the warriors, men and women, who struggle near me, almost touching my head. . . . Quite near an Apsara smiles upon me from the melée. Hers is the last image of which I am conscious. For some seconds longer I see her fair breast gleaming, looking moist as if it were beaded with a warm sweat, . . . and then, no more; I lapse into unconsciousness.

I have been asleep for an hour, perhaps, when one of my Siamese servants brings me the cards of three visitors. The names are French. Yes, by all means show them in—even here, into my splendid reception hall. But truly, it is the last thing I should have expected: to receive visitors at Angkor.

Three Frenchmen in fact. They have been sent to Siam in pursuance of archæological studies, and since yesterday have been installed, not far from me, beneath a roof of thatch in the holy enclosure. They are learned and agreeable. Besides, after days of solitude and silence, travelling without companions, it is a relief to exchange thoughts with men of France.

AN APSARA

Siam

1 ought to remain, they tell me, for the forest is full of unknown ruins. Over and above the great temples which every one visits, there are to be found scattered about, by the side of the rivers and swamps, a number of monuments in terra cotta of an art most singular, dating back to the fourth century, and even to the earliest days of the Khmer Empire.

But no; I will adhere to my intention of leaving to-day in the decline of the sun. First, there are the elephants of the good King Norodom which I am due to meet the day after to-morrow at Kompong-Luong. And then, and more especially, how should I forget that I am, in fact, no more than a modest aide-de-camp, whose leave is limited, and must report myself, within the stipulated time, on board the war-ship which awaits me at Saigon?

I have given the order to prepare our departure for five o'clock; and, while the ox-carts are being got ready and my kit is being packed, I mount the steps of the temple for the last time.

No rain has fallen since last night to refresh the suspended plants, or moisten the heaps of stones, and an intolerable heat, as of glowing

coal, now emanates from the terraces, the walls
and statuary, on which the sun has been blazing
all day long. But the divine Apsaras, who
have been used for centuries to be thus burnt
with rays, smile at me by way of adieu, without losing their ease or customary gracious
irony. As I took leave of them I little thought
that within a few hours, by the lavish caprice
of the King of Pnom-Penh, I should see them
again, one night, at the evocation of the sound
of the old music of their times, see them no
longer dead, with these fixed smiles of stone,
but in the fulness of life and youth, no longer
with these breasts of rigid sandstone, but with
palpitating breasts of flesh, and coifed in veritable tiaras of gold, and sparkling with veritable
jewels. . . .

The sun is already low in the heavens and
beginning to cast a ruddy light when my
little train of ox-carts gets under way, leaving
Angkor behind for ever, along the paved causeway, between the bushes clustered with the
white bloom of the fragrant jasmine. Beyond
the large pools choked with weeds and water-
lilies, beyond the bridge, the last porticoes and
the great seven-headed serpents which guard the

Siam

threshold, the pathway of departure opens before us. It plunges under the trees which are ready at once to hide the great temple from us. I turn, therefore, to take a last look at Angkor. This pilgrimage, which, since my childhood, I had hoped to make, is now a thing accomplished, fallen into the past, as soon will fall my own brief human existence, and I shall never see again, rising into the sky, those great strange towers. I cannot even, this last time, follow them for long with my eyes, for very quickly the forest closes round us, ushering in a sudden twilight.

At about seven or eight o'clock we reach the Siamese village of Siem-Reap, on the bank of the river, in the region of the tall palms. It is quite dark, and the half-naked folk who move about under the vault of trees get the light they need by waving burning brands, as is the custom also in India on the Malabar coast. They hasten to welcome us and instal us, on the river bank, in a hut used by the travelling pilgrims, which seems to be on stilts, so high are the piles on which it is raised.

CHAPTER X

CHAPTER X

Sunday, 1st December 1901.

AN hour more in our ox-carts, along the bank of the little river, in the freshness of the early morning, passing through Eden-like villages, amongst palms and garlands of blossoming creepers.

At a point on the bank the sampan which brought us hither is awaiting us—the large sampan, the roof of which is in the form of a coffin lid. Then, leaving our carts, we begin to descend the narrow river, brushed by reeds, by grasses of gigantic size. First of all, swamps gradually getting more and more inundated, and then the submerged forest, which, as it envelops us in its poisonous shadow, takes away the little respirable air there was. An hour and a half is spent in traversing the gloomy labyrinth, rowing between enormous half-submerged trees, amongst branches entangled with creepers. It is not till about mid-day that we escape from the oppression of the forest and that the great lake, opening at last ahead of us, unrolls before our eyes, which are dazzled at the sight, its wide expanse as of a sea of gleaming tin.

The steamboat, which is to take us back to Cambodia, is there, moored to the branches of this semblance of a shore, looking as if it were lost in the midst of this desert of verdure and warm water. Let us get up steam and depart as soon as possible.

All the afternoon, all the evening, is spent in gliding, with rapid and monotonous motion, over this lake which to-day has no visible limits, to such a degree does the evaporated moisture blot out the horizon. The sun seems to vaporise it, to drink it—a sun that, all imbued with moisture as it is, itself looks troubled, though, nevertheless, sinister and terrible. Not a breath anywhere, and a mortal electric tension. Our steamboat makes little ridges on the mournful water, ridges always alike, which disappear in silence in ever-lessening ripples. We seem to be sailing on some mysterious molten metal, too sluggish or too heavy for such noise as ordinary water makes; and thus the companies of pelicans we rock in our passage, asleep in long bands of pinkish-white, are scarcely disturbed by our approach. Everywhere, somnolence and torpor under a light at once excessive and diffuse. From time to time there are enacted before us phantasmagorias that seem designed to scare us: they appear always in the direction of the west. We see sombre things rising in the distance, almost as quickly as the dense smoke of volcanoes. They darken a whole side of the sky; they take on shades of copper; they assume the appearance of toppling rocks, of mountains about to tumble into chaos: rough shapings of storms which do not break, but are transformed at once, dissolving and vanishing like the visions of dreams.

Not a boat in sight, not a canoe: we are alone upon this shoreless sea. Through all these insubstantialities of air and water, without any kind of landmark, our pilot—a Siamese—guides himself by instinct, no doubt, in the same way as the migrating birds. In the twilight, however, when he is endeavouring to find the entrance to the river down which our further course lies, he is perplexed, he hesitates and changes his route. There is no danger, however, only the risk of being detained here till daybreak.

And now night falls, moist and languorous, and we scarcely know where we are. The water has not always clear contours. Dark masses, which are really storm clouds, resemble in places adjacent banks. We see rising phantoms of mountains, phantoms of forests.

Pale stars, bedimmed as was the sun, appear at last through the mist to guide us. Our pilot thinks he has found his bearings, and we continue on our way at full speed. A violent shock! The boat rears and stops, while at the same time the air is rent with the sound of breaking branches. A mass of shadow, which he had taken for one of the deceptive clouds, proves to be really the bank; we have plunged into it, our bows sheer amongst the trees, and from the concussion a thousand little beasts, which were asleep in the verdure, descend like a rain upon us, locusts, beetles, lizards, and venomous little snakes. The engines are reversed, and we extricate ourselves without having suffered damage. We had struck only soft mud and fragile mangroves. And our Siamese, it appears, had missed the entrance to the river by only a few yards, so that soon we find it, and, sure of our way, proceed with speed accelerated now by the current. It is the Mekong at last, and we prepare to sleep, satisfied that all is for the best.

CHAPTER XI

CHAPTER XI

Monday, 2nd December 1901.

AT about three o'clock this morning, under a deluge in which all the clouds of yesterday were emptying themselves, we had come to a mooring amongst the reeds of the great river, near the village of Kompong-Luong. It is here that the river brings me nearest to a certain temple dedicated to the manes of the queen-mother of Cambodia, to which I intend, in passing, to make a pilgrimage. It lies some distance away in the dense bush.

Now, at daybreak, I am awakened by formidable footsteps, which make the adjacent bank tremble, and are accompanied by a music of breaking branches. Through a porthole, open near my head, I look to see what ponderous visitors attend me. The just dawning day reveals to me a medley of reeds and moistened bushes, which already seem too vividly green for so dim a light, just as the

141

sun, too, seems too red. And in this setting of the early morning colossal beasts appear, gambolling in clumsy playfulness, and shaking the earth. It might be some scene of the earliest ages of the world. These elephants—for elephants they are—are doubtless the four promised by King Norodom, and they are come punctually to the rendezvous. Four men, clothed in white, follow them, talking to them with a sort of quiet patience, and at an order given almost in a whisper, they become motionless right opposite to me.

When the good elephants are saddled, having each on its nape a squatting driver, and on its back a palanquin like a Cambodian cabin, I am invited to take my place, with my interpreter and my two servants. We set off in line, each of us in his little oscillating hut. We have to go, first of all, through the village. Then the market, where a world of little yellow folk is busy at its bargaining, buying and selling fruits, grains, chickens, and strange-looking fish from the Mekong. Our elephants, aware of the fear they are about to cause, walk here with only short, quiet steps, but, as invariably happens, all the oxen, all the buffaloes flee before the sovereign beast, and

Siam

some mannikins are knocked over, some bowls of milk upset—there are cries, tumult.

After this isolated grouping of humanity, we plunge for two or three hours into the dense bush, and meet not a soul on our way. There is no forest of shadows here as in Siam, but simply bush, that Indo - Chinese bush, inextricable, always the same, useless and endless. We follow narrow pathways, on a soil of the red of bloodstone, between two curtains of bushes of most brilliant green. Foliage which is strange to us imprisons us more and more in its multitudinous compactness: a whole vegetation eternally watered, eternally overheated, which yet does not succeed in attaining any height of growth, but remains dwarfish and soft and of an unhealthy exuberance. From the vantage of our palanquins we see from time to time unlimited expanses of this mournful verdure, which tells of exile and savours of fever.

In the foreground, in front of me, always the bronze neck of the elephant-driver, and now and then, two enormous grey ears which rise and beat the air like fans. One has a sense of princely well-being in the little rocking cabin, sheltered from the sun of fire, travelling in this sure and solid fashion, with a step that never stumbles, and a smoothness that no obstacle will have the force to disturb. And yet in time the heart begins to sicken a little at the monotony of this bush which closes behind you in silence, ceaselessly, mercilessly, as the minutes pass.

We make our mid-day halt at an old monastery at the foot of a little mountain, which serves as a pedestal to the mausoleum of the Cambodian kings. Here there is some running water and trees that are really tall, and we seem to have hit upon a little corner of paradise in the midst of this desert of noxious verdure. A vast hall of reddish-coloured wood, with a fantastic roof, having by way of walls little more than reed blinds, and by way of decoration huge Buddhist pictures on rice paper, which are suspended from the pillars. We instal ourselves there on mats, welcomed, with fitting dignity, by two or three venerable monks, and a very aged woman, with white close-cropped hair, whose face of parchment bears the impress of a hundred years. Our elephants have been let loose in the bush, where they will eat for their dinner a few young trees. Treading on tip-toe, the venerable old lady in her religious garb of yellow brings us square-shaped cushions on which to recline or lay our head. She says nothing, and her features, transfixed by so many years of a mysticism unintelligible to our souls, do not move. After the mid-day repast we fall asleep, stretched on our mats, in a peculiar kind of monachal peace, broken only by the sound of the neighbouring stream, which gives an illusion of coolness.

About half-past three comes the awakening, for my attendants as well as for myself, and I order the elephants to be brought back, for it is the hour to resume our journey.

This mountain which overhangs the monastery is one of those geological fantasies which are scattered here and there in the midst of the low-lying plains of Cambodia: one of those abrupt, isolated, unexpected cones which are known here as *pnôm*. They one nearly all deemed holy, and serve as a base to a place of prayer. This particular one, already very pointed in itself, is made more so by the mausoleum which caps it and is more pointed, more slender than any of our cathedral spires. And it is there, high above the jungle infested with tigers and monkeys, which surrounds it, as near as possible to the storm-filled sky, that the old kings of Cambodia sleep. The ashes of the queen-mother have been deposited there recently after a cremation attended with immemorial rites, with a ceremonial of dance and music dating back beyond all doubt to the days of Angkor.

It is about an hour's journey from the monastery to the pagoda consecrated to the manes of this old princess, which is the goal of my pilgrimage. The sun is getting low when we perceive it, in a kind of glade in the midst of the bush. Amongst tall, slender palm-trees, the green plumes of which dominate the surrounding jungle, it appears before us all illuminated by the Bengal lights of the setting sun, its tarnished gildings gleaming softly like some precious piece of antique jewellery. Its image is reflected in a solitary pool strewn with eyots of pink lotus. It is ornamented, needless to say, with long, golden horns, which part in all directions from the roof; and it stands on a triple-staged pedestal, on the ledges of which monsters, in attitudes of mockery, are consumed with laughter, with the horrible laughter of a death's head. Hearing our elephants approaching, some of the monks, robed in lemon-yellow and draped in orange-yellow, open the doors and stand in staged groups on the steps of the threshold. It is truly a perfect vision of the old ages of Asia that was awaiting us in the silence of this remote spot and in the red glow of evening.

I am advised by my interpreter that it would be more discreet on my part, and more correct, not to ask the monks, who would not venture to refuse me, for permission to visit the interior of the pagoda. Without descending from my palanquin, I confine myself, therefore, to the slow circuit of its base.

It is the art of Angkor that one finds again here, greatly reduced, of course, from its colossal proportions, and a little too affected, perhaps, too mannered, but yet of a most exquisite strangeness. At Angkor the enormous walls were covered with embroideries of stone. Here, beneath the fantastic roof with its great golden horns, the pagoda seems to be hung with a sumptuous old brocade, which scintillates in the dying rays of the sun—it is a veritable network of minute carvings in gilded stucco, in which are mingled particles of crystal imitating rubies and emeralds. And the doors, which shine with a different and bluish lustre, are in mosaic of mother-of-pearl.

Siam

Our elephants, as if they realised that we wished to view the pagoda without haste, make the circuit of the terraces with a somnolent majesty. One after another, each of the statues, placed on the ledges of the pedestal, presents to us, as we pass, its grimace of irony. They have the bodies of men, but the faces of scarecrows; they represent the guardian spirits of the eternal thresholds; and their presence suffices to mark a place of funeral and to command reflection. Standing there, with legs apart and hands resting on their bent knees, they look as if they stooped thus in a convulsion of laughter —laughing at the transiency of human things, no doubt, laughing at birth and laughing at death. As in the case of the walls of the pagoda, the monsters which guard it are covered with gilded carvings and facets of crystal, which make for them costumes of great pomp and show, a little faded, it is true, and spotted with grey mouldiness. As for their faces, they are already familiar to us; they have been copied from the thousand-year-old bas-reliefs of Angkor. But why these convulsed attitudes of uncanny laughter in this place of final and abiding peace? To us what an abysm of mystery there is in such a conception of tombs!

Siam

When we have completed the circuit of the
pagoda, and return once more before the doors
of mother-of-pearl, it is only the gold of the
roof, its somewhat Chinese curves and its long
horns which shine with a bright effulgence.
The sun has buried itself in the endless verdure
of the plains. It no longer illumines the walls,
and we see these old brocades, already faded
by the rains of many seasons, dimmed with
subtle shadings, and dappled, in places only, by
a kind of embroidery of crystal. The monks
—to do us honour—have remained standing on
the steps. And the whole picture—the pagoda,
these motionless people in yellow robes, the
funereal spirits laughing on the ledges of the
terraces, with hands resting on their outspread
knees — is reflected in the dead waters of
the pond, where the lotus, flowers of broad
day, are beginning to close and seal their
pink petals because the shadows of evening
are falling. And upon these superannuated
splendours there seems to descend more and
more, as the twilight deepens, the peace of profound isolation.

It is the hour of departure, and the pace of
our elephants quickens for the return journey.
We plunge again into the narrow pathways,

where we are encompassed and brushed continually by the verdure. Once more the bush closes behind us, the eternal bush, hastening to hide from us the magic glade, which, perhaps, is haunted occasionally still by the incomprehensible soul of a queen of furthest Asia.

Dark night when the good giant beasts kneel down to deposit us at the village of the morning, near the bank of the river. The boat is awaiting us there under steam, and I prepare at once to continue the journey down the Mekong. It is the time of the year when the waters of the lakes of Siam are emptied into the great river, and we set out with all the speed of our engines added to the swiftness of the current. Soon after midnight we have reached Pnom-Penh, and are moored before the gardens of the Governor.

CHAPTER XII

CHAPTER XII

Tuesday, 3rd December 1901.

AT Pnom - Penh until the midnight follow -
ing, after which it will be necessary to fall
back upon Saigon, so as to report myself on
board at the expiration of my leave. A warm,
torrential rain the whole day long.

This evening at nine o'clock old King Norodom
is to receive me. And the Governor, having had
the great kindness to intimate to him that I
was not an ordinary aide-de-camp, but a *lettré
de France*, it appears that there is to be a
grand reception in which the *corps de ballet* of
the court will figure.

The rain is still falling in a deluge when the
Governor's carriage comes to take me to the
palace. The night is suffocating, in spite of
the tropical downpour which descends upon us
from the black sky. Our way lies under confused trees, along dark avenues where nothing
seems to be alive. But a blaze of light greets

Siam

us on arrival, and attendants, carrying large Asiatic umbrellas, hurry forward to assist us in alighting, and to shelter us in our passage to the reception hall.

It is immense, this hall, but it has no walls, nothing but a roof upheld in the air by very tall blue pillars. In the girandoles and on the silver Cambodian torches—where not long ago burnt only wicks soaked in oil—electric light has recently been installed. It is a little disconcerting here, and splashes with brutality the crowd of princesses, ladies-in-waiting, attendants, musicians, some five or six hundred people in all, who are seated on mats on the floor. All the costumes are white and all the draperies, and there is a multitude of bare arms and bare bosoms of the colour of pale bronze. The orchestra, as soon as we appear, begins a music of Asia, which straightaway transports us into far distances of space and time. It is slow and loud, rendered by some thirty instruments of metal or resonant wood, which are struck with velvet-topped batons. There are dulcimers, wooden harmonicas with a very extended keyboard, and peals of little gongs which vibrate in the manner of pianos played with the loud pedal. The melody is infinitely sad, but the rhythm gets more and more rapid until it reaches a kind of frenzy, like the rhythm of a tarantella.

We are escorted to a platform and bidden seat ourselves near the golden-mattressed couch on which presently the old, infirm, and almost dying king will come to lie. Near us, on a gilt table, are cups of champagne, and boxes, made of the reddish gold of Cambodia, filled with cigarettes. We command the hall, of which the centre, carpeted with white mats and large enough for the manœuvring of a battalion, is empty. It is there that the spectacle of the ballet will be presented to us. Very large Chinese vases, containing drenched foliage variegated like flowers, are placed at the foot of each of the pillars. Between the pillars, above the white-clothed crowd, are revealed the black of the rainy night, the darkness of the profound sky ; and, above all, the rain which is now descending in torrents more furious than ever. The smallest drops, in passing into the vivid electric light, sparkle with prismatic lights, sparkle so that one seems to see precious stones falling in thousands, diamonds in cascades. Two doors at the further end open into the interior of the palace, and it is from these that the ballerinas will appear. The heat remains over-powering, in spite of the large fans which are waved unceasingly above our heads by the attendants. And everywhere flights of insects, maddened by the brilliance of the girandoles, whirl innumerable; mosquitoes, day-flies, humming beetles, and large moths.

The king is long in coming, and presently attendants bring his crown and sceptre of gold, set with large rubies and emeralds, and place them on a cushion near us. He is after all too ill to appear;[1] he begs that we will excuse him, and send us these attributes of sovereignty to intimate to us that the reception is, nevertheless, a royal one.

The spectacle, then, will begin without him. The music suddenly becomes quieter and more mysterious, as if it were announcing something supernatural. One of the doors at the back opens; an adorable and almost fantastic little creature springs into the middle of the hall—an Apsara of the temple of Angkor! It would be impossible to imagine an illusion

---

[1] He died a short time afterwards. And it is his successor, King Sisovath, who visited France, and committed the amiable fault of showing to the Parisians some of the ballerinas of his court. One ought not to profane and diminish such spectacles by producing them in this way out of their proper frame.

Siam

more perfect. She has the same features because she is of the same unmingled blood, the same enigmatic smile, the eyes downcast, almost closed, the same breast of budding womanhood, scarcely veiled by a thin network of silk. And her costume is scrupulously copied from the old bas-reliefs, but copied in real jewels, in gorgeous fabrics; kinds of sheathes of gold brocade imprison her legs and loins. Her face whitened with fard, her eyes artificially elongated, she wears a very high tiara of gold, studded with rubies, which tapers to a point like the roof of a pagoda, and on either shoulder a kind of pinion, like a dolphin's fin, in gold and precious stones. Of gold likewise, set with precious stones, are the broad waistband, the rings which ornament her ankles and her bare arms of amber-colour faintly flushed with pink.

Alone at first upon the scene, this little Apsara of remote ages, escaped from the sacred bas-relief, makes signs of appeal in the direction of the door of the background — which has become for us the door of fairy-like apparitions— and two of her sisters run out to join her, two new Apsaras, likewise sparkling, their hips moulded in the same rigid sheathes, wearing the same golden crowns and the same golden pinions. All three join hands. They are the queens of the Apsaras, doubtless, for a throne has been prepared for them. But they exchange a mimicry of anxiety, and begin again to make signs of appeal, always in the direction of that same door. . . . We have already marvelled at seeing three. Can it be that there are others still to come ? And now they appear in groups, ten, twenty, thirty, decked like goddesses as were the first, wearing on their charming heads and shoulders all the treasure of Cambodia.

Before the three enthroned queens, they proceed to perform their ritual dances, which involve little or no change of place, but consist rather in rhythmic movements or quiverings of the whole body. They undulate like snakes, these slender little creatures, their exquisitely muscular bodies seeming to be without bone. At times they spread out their arms in the form of a cross, and then the serpentine undulation begins in the fingers of the right hand, flows through the wrist, the fore arm, the elbow, the shoulder, crosses the breast, and continues on the opposite side, following the other arm until it dies at last on the tips of the fingers of the left hand, overloaded with rings.

In real life these exquisite little ballerinas

are very jealously guarded, are often indeed princesses of the royal blood, whom no one has the right either to approach or gaze upon. They have been trained from their earliest years to these movements which do not seem possible for human limbs ; to these poses which are so little natural, but are, nevertheless, of immemorial tradition in this country, as is proved by the stone personages who inhabit the ruins.

They are going to mime now some scenes from the Ramayana, such as formerly were carved in hard sandstone, in the bas - reliefs of the ancestral temple. The handsome war-chariots, copied in little from those of Angkor, make their entry. But, by a naïve convention, the elephants which should be drawing them have been replaced by men, walking on all fours, naked and yellow, masked in huge cardboard heads with moveable trunks and ears. Then we assist at divers episodes, pleasant and tragic, at combats between monsters, above all at the filing past of processions in celebration of victories. We see a little queen, of fourteen or fifteen years, very much bejewelled, very much painted, ideal in her war-chariot, pursued by the declarations of love of a young warrior, and repulsing them with a grace infinitely chaste. We see a thousand subtle and charming things which testify to an art of the most refined kind. Whenever a train of Apsaras retires by one of the doors of the background, another train enters from another door and proceeds slowly to occupy the hall. There are some of them, some of these little fairies all in gold, who can be no more than seven or eight years old; and they file past, painted like idols, crowned with very high tiaras, with jewelled pinions on their shoulders, grave and dignified in hieratic attitudes.

A heat more and more oppressive is exhaled from this crowd, which is perfumed with musk and flowers; the torrential rain continues to fill the background of the picture with its stream of sparkling gems; from all the neighbouring bush, myriads of little winged beasts come without ceasing to hurl themselves upon the lustres and torches; there come, too, large bats and nocturnal birds; the exuberant animal life, with which the air is filled to excess, envelops us and penetrates us.

And now enters the "King of the Monkeys," grimacing, in his mask of gold—just as I have seen him, needless to say, in the bas-reliefs of

the old temple. He also assumes poses which
are not natural, are not possible (the poses of
the bas-reliefs, always); his youthful limbs
have been adapted from very early days to
these exigencies of tradition. In his train the
whole army of monkeys invades the scene :
young girls again, little princesses masked like
scarecrows, but whose rising breasts are outlined underneath the flimsy coverings of costly
silks. And the business is, for this astonishing
but little redoubtable cohort to go to the rescue
of fair Sita, whom the demons hold captive,
a very long way off, on an island. . . . We are
in the midst of the Ramayana, and the same
spectacles were once enacted, no doubt, at
Angkor-Thom, the same costumes were worn
there. This evening I am able to imagine,
better than ever before, what were the splendours
of the old legendary town. Days that we
thought were dead and done for ever come
to life again before our eyes. But it is no
effort of the imagination which thus recon-
stitutes them. The simple truth is that nothing
has changed here, whether in the souls of men
or in the secrets of palaces, since the heroic
ages. In spite of its diminished outward
seeming, this fallen Cambodian people has

remained the Khmer people, the people which astonished the Asia of olden times by its pomp and mysticism. One knows, too, that it has never surrendered its hope of reconquering its great capital, buried for centuries now in the forests of Siam; and it is always the Ramayana, that epic so ancient and so nebulous, which continues to haunt its imagination and to direct its dream.

Let us hope that France, the protectress (?) of this land, may be able to understand that the ballet of the kings of Pnom-Penh is a sacred heritage, a marvel of antiquity not to be destroyed!

At about one o'clock in the morning, in dark night and under a warm rain, we leave the palace of Norodom, and I go at once to have the steamboat, which awaits me, made ready for departure. I recommence to descend the current of the Mekong, in deep and oppressive darkness, and the vision of the little fairies of the Ramayana vanishes from me.

The day after to-morrow must find me back at Saigon, that baleful town of languor and death, to take my place again in attendance on the admiral, amongst my companions in exile;

Siam

to shut myself up once more within the stifling
iron walls of that warship, which, for nearly
two-and-twenty months, has carried us through
all the swells of the seas of China, but which
sleeps now alongside the unhealthy quay, where
the verdure of the trees is too vividly green,
and the soil of mournful redness.

CHAPTER XIII

CHAPTER XIII

NEARLY ten more years have passed since my pilgrimage. And now the hour has come, quickly, stealthily, the hour which it seemed to me should never come, the twilight hour of life when all earthly things grow distant, diminish, and are blurred with grey shadows.

After a luminous summer, perhaps the last, spent in the East, I am back again, since this morning, in my parental home. It is fine to-day in this corner of France on which my eyes opened, fine and calm under a blue sky; but the sun, which yet is clear and warm, has a touch of paleness, which betokens the decline of the season and adds to the melancholy of my return.

And here now has chance brought me back to this little retreat which was the museum of my childhood — a little room of which I scarcely thought ever again to open the door,

Siam

but which I allowed to subsist as a place of
memory. The poor things, which once so filled
my mind with thoughts of distant countries,
are withering and crumbling in their little glass
cases, like mummies neglected in their hypogeum.
There is a faded odour of camphor, of stuffed
birds, an indefinable savour of mortality, and
it is sad here, this evening, unspeakably. I
open the window. . . . But it seems to me
that everything becomes more mournful still
when I let in the rays of the sun of this
October evening. And, see ! a wasp has entered
at the same time. . . . I remember how in
the old days many a wasp used to enter thus,
for the little room opens on to the gardens,
on to the old country gardens, the walls of
which are tapestried with vines and rose-
trees.

I think of it suddenly, that out-of-date copy
of a colonial review containing the pictures
which were the first to reveal to me the ruins
of Angkor ! It should still be there, behind
that curtain. How is it that it did not occur
to me to look for it on my return from Asia ?
I try to find it now in this recess, where the
dust lies thick like an impalpable ash.

It was certainly decisive, the influence this

museum exercised in the orientation of my life.
It happens so for the majority of men, simple
playthings as they are of their first impressions;
trifles long dwelt upon in childhood suffice to
sway, one way or another, the whole sequence
of their destiny; and this evening—is it because
I have not seen it for so many months, my
tiny museum? — this evening its spell still
works. The poor things on its shelves induce
in me almost the hankering and the thrill ot
unknown countries, calling me to escape and
come to them. How childish the feeling is!
It is finished, all that; the unknown exists
no longer, and I have drained the cup ot
adventures to the dregs. The gaily-coloured
bird behind this glass once made me dream
of "colonies," but I have wandered in the
most impenetrable of the forests in which it
dwells. That humble calabash, with its barbarous
designs, I used to deem a precious curiosity,
but I have lived amongst the black Yoloffs
who excel in carving them thus, in the shadow
of their reed roofs, before their horizons of
sand. That paddle, hanging on the wall, once
conjured up visions of savage islanders, but the
Polynesians have taught me how to manipulate
identical things, in companionship with them,

in canoes rocked in the swell of the great ocean. . . . Is that, then, all the world is? Is human life no more than that?

Ah! I have found the copy of the colonial review containing the revelation of Angkor. How imperfect and ill-drawn the pictures seem on this yellowed paper, compared with the admirable illustrations we are used to to-day! Alas, they date back some half-century. They are very faithful, nevertheless, and show clearly the tall turrets, in outline like tiaras, which I have since seen in reality, alike under the tropical sun and under lowering storm clouds. And as I gaze upon these unpretentious little drawings, immediately — need I say it? — the impressions of that far off April evening crowd back into my memory. Even those emphatic phrases of Ecclesiastes, which then sang themselves in my childish head, come back as if they were of yesterday: "I have tried all things, I have been everywhere. . . . In the depths of the forests of Siam I have seen the star of evening rise over the ruins of mysterious Angkor. . . ."

And to-day! Yes, it is the day of that mournful return home of which I had so clear a presentiment, the last return of all, with heart aweary and whitening hair. The fact admits of no disguise; the day has come, the cycle of my life is closed.

The wasps continue to invade my little room, wasps and buzzing flies; before the little sealed glass-cases and the little dead things, they describe their foolish curves. The time is near, however, when they will go to sleep or die; but they, too, have no doubt felt the influence of tradition, that they come thus merrily to renew acquaintance with a place which has so long been closed, where they used formerly to dance their whirligigs in my company. The smallest insects, so they say, repeat eternally the same things in the same places, just as the tiny mosses and wild flowerets live and live again for centuries in the same corner of the wood.

To turn over the leaves of this ancient, out-of-date review, I have seated myself near the open window. The late October sun is sinking over the plain of Aunis which I can see beyond the neighbouring roofs and the ramparts. On the limit of the horizon there are still the same woods, adjoining those of Limoise, and the line of their configuration has not been changed. In the distance, amidst the meadows,

the Charente traces its slender, shining track—
and formerly this river by which the ships made
their way to foreign countries, to the "colonies,"
represented for me the gateway into the unknown; but where would it lead me now, to
what oceans that I have not explored? In
the review resting on my knee, I discover
pictures which I had not noticed or had forgotten: here is the great mask of Brahma,
such as it appeared to me one evening in the
forest of shadow, multiplied in startling fashion,
and gazing down upon me from the height of
the quadruple-visaged towers. I did not suspect
that it had been lying in wait for me so many
years, on a dusty shelf, amongst the familiar
toys of my childhood. On the next page are
three Apsaras of the bas-reliefs, with rounded
bosoms copied from models which throbbed a
thousand years ago. They take me back in
spirit to the ballet of the kings of Pnom-Penh,
which was, as it were, the apotheosis of my
pilgrimage, a veritable blaze of gold and colour
and light, scarcely imaginable here amid this
peaceful setting of autumn in my native province, while the last wasps of summer are
buzzing idly round me. My inattentive eyes
wander from the pages I am turning over to

the horizon, filled now with a golden sadness by the setting sun. If nothing has changed in my museum of yore, so, too, has everything remained unaltered in this part of my native town, which is falling more and more into desuetude, as its maritime activity is little by little being withdrawn. The same stretches of wall, covered with the same jasmine and creepers; the same Roman-tiled roofs, turning yellow with the rust of time; the same chimneys whose every outline I recognise so well against the sky of this close of an autumn day. The trees of the gardens, which were already old when I began to live, have not grown sensibly older since. The great elms of the ramparts, which even then were centenarian, are still there, forming a girdle as magnificent as ever with their same green tufts. And when everything around has preserved itself unchanged, how difficult it is to imagine, how hard to admit, that I myself am nearly done with, simply because I shall soon attain the number of years allotted, without mercy, to the average of existences. Heavens! to finish when you feel that nothing in you has changed, and that the same zest for adventure, the same hunger after the unknown would possess you still, did but

the cause remain! Is it possible, alas! in the
presence of this simple but unchanging scene
which ought, one might think, to envelop you
in a kind of protection, to impregnate you a
little with its faculty of duration, is it possible
in the presence of all this which perpetuates
itself so easily, to have been a child for whom
the world is about to open, to have been that
which has its life to live, and to become at last
no more than that which has lived its life?

And, nevertheless, out of my short life,
scattered about over the whole world, I shall
have extracted something, a kind of lore which
does not yet suffice, but has brought already
a promise of serenity. In my travels, I have
seen so many places of passionate adoration,
each one responding to a particular form of
the human agony, so many pagodas, so many
mosques, so many cathedrals, where the same
prayer has been poured forth from the depths
of hearts the most diverse! These things have
not only disclosed to me that cold half-proof
of the existence of a God which was indicated
in the philosophical courses of my youth, and
to-day is mere idle repetition: "the proof by
the unanimous consent of mankind." Not only
that, but something infinitely more important,

namely, that such a chorus of supplications, such a widespread testimony of burning tears imply the almost universal confidence that this God cannot be other than a God of pity. Nay, let it not be thought that I am pretending to say a thing that is the least bit new. I only wish to add mine to the thousand other testimonies, in the thought that it may be of interest, perhaps, to some amongst my fellows. In proportion as the centuries accumulated on humanity, the savage gods which it had imagined on its first issue from original darkness gave place to conceptions more gentle, less gross, and, surely, nearer to the truth. In proportion as the love of one for another, the brotherly love preached by Buddha and by Jesus, made its way into our souls, prone naturally to more savage tendencies, the notion strengthened in us that there must be somewhere a Supreme Pity that would hear our cries,—and then the sanctuaries became more and more places of supplication and of tears. In the mosques of Islam, from Moghreb to Mecca, never a day passes but innumerable men, the forehead beating the gound, appeal to the mercy of Allah! The jealous and gloomy Jehovah of the Hebrews has been effaced before the advent

Siam

of Christ, and I have seen the Holy Sepulchre which is the place in all the world where the sobs of trustful supplicants may most be heard. Even at Angkor, Buddhist statues, with a smile of pardon, are seated before the four doors of the immured cella in which men, even so long as a thousand years ago, felt that it was necessary to hide the terrible God of their first theogonies. More and more am I fain to believe in the Sovereign Pity, to stretch out my arms towards it, because I have suffered so much, under diverse skies, amid enchantments and amid horrors, and because I have seen so much suffering, seen so many tears, so many prayers. In spite of fluctuations, in spite of vicissitudes, in spite of revolts caused by too strict dogmas and exclusive formulæ, one feels the existence of this Sovereign Pity affirmed more and more universally in the lofty souls who are enlightened by the great new lights which break upon the world.[1]

---

[1] In France, our admirable Bergson, who has overthrown determinism ; in America, William James and the disciples who follow him ; in India, a few wise men of Benares and Hadyar. On the one side by irrefutable logic, on the other by marvellous observation, all to-day are coming little by little to consolidate those hopes, which our ancestors, without so much seeking, were able to discover so surely and so naturally behind the symbols of the intuitive religions.

Siam

Nowadays, it is true, we have amongst us that lees of half-intelligences, of minds partially instructed, which the social régime of our time causes to rise to the surface, and which, in the name of science, rushes without understanding into the most imbecile materialism. But, in the progressive evolution, the reign of these feeble souls will mark only a negligible episode of retrogression. The Supreme Pity towards which we stretch out despairing hands is a necessity of our existence, by whatever name we may call it; it is necessary that it should be there, capable of hearing, at the moment of the visitations of death, our clamour of infinite distress. For without it the Creation, to which one can no longer reasonably ascribe incognizance as an excuse, would become a cruelty too unthinkable, it would be so odious and so cowardly.

And out of my numberless pilgrimages, those that were frivolous and those that were grave, this feeble argument, so little new as it is, is all of value that I have been able to carry away.

INDEX

Index

Index

Index

For Product Safety Concerns and Information please contact our EU
representative GPSR@taylorandfrancis.com Taylor & Francis Verlag GmbH,
Kaufingerstraße 24, 80331 München, Germany

Batch number: 08165901

Printed by Printforce, the Netherlands